ESSENCE OF INQUIRY
VICHARASANGRAHAM

A COMMENTARY BY
NOME

Published by
Society of Abidance in Truth (SAT)
1834 Ocean Street
Santa Cruz, CA 95060 USA
web: www.SATRamana.org
email: sat@satramana.org

CONTENTS

FOREWORD

Ramana has been variously described though he is the One beyond description. For all descriptions are, after all, mental and cannot grasp the nature and stature of the infinite Ramana. Some describe him as "Maharshi," an adjective made popular by Paul Brunton in the West. "Rishi" means a seer of truth, and "Maharshi" means a prominent rishi. What such a one teaches or explains is from a direct perception of truth without the superimposition of mental concepts and ideas. Hence, the teaching has a universal and timeless validity. Ramana is also called "Bhagavan" or "God." The reason for this is not far to see, for Ramana was always steadfast in his state of steady bliss, of natural samadhi. Radiating grace and power, he lived a perfect life unbound by time and space, as an example for all humanity to follow. People who moved closely with Ramana for many years asserted that one like him "comes only once in a millennium or two."

Vicharasangraham, Self-Inquiry, was Ramana's first original work. It is in the form of a dialogue, a question and answer session between Sadguru Ramana and an ardent seeker of truth, Gambhiram Seshayya (also known as Seshiah). It took place in the beginning of the twentieth century between 1900 and 1902 at Tiruvannamalai, India. At that time, Ramana was observing silence not because of any mental resolve but simply because he did not feel the urge to speak. However, since the purpose of his advent was to be a universal teacher, no one was denied guidance. Fortunately, the questions and answers were contemporaneously recorded by Seshayya on slips of paper, which he subsequently noted in a dairy. This has been preserved for posterity. The work is, therefore, an authentic record of Ramana's teachings.

The format—questions and answers—is time honored and makes for easy understanding. Though this is the first original work of Ramana, unfortunately it has taken a back seat because the questioner was following path of raja yoga. To do so would be to overlook the fact that such ones like Ramana come to "fulfill, not to destroy." Ramana did not condemn any of the extant practices, for each has a role in one's spiritual growth, a role in preparing one for the straight and royal path of self-inquiry taught by Ramana. While clarifying the doubts of Seshayya, Ramana would always bring him back to the importance of inquiry about the subject, about the "I," about "nonobjective," holistic, spiritual practice. In no other work do we find such a clear, lucid exposition of the nature of the mind.

To write a commentary on the sacred words of Ramana, one has to be constantly perceptive of his ever-flowing grace. It is evident Master Nome has this perception. The humility with which he has approached this holy work is found in his beginning each commentary with the all-powerful twelve syllable mantra on Ramana "Om Namo Bhagavate Sri Ramanaya." He closes each commentary with "Om Sri Ramanarpanamastu—Om may this be an offering to Sri Ramana." And what worthy offering it is. With his own experience of the natural state, Nome is able to explain the true import of Ramana's word with utmost clarity and depth. A brief look at one of the commentaries indicates this:

Question number 2

Disciple: What is meant by saying that one should enquire into one's nature?

The Maharshi: Experience such as "I went," "I came," "I did," comes naturally to everyone. From these experiences, does it not appear that the consciousness "I" is the subject of those various acts? Enquiring into the true nature of that consciousness and remaining as oneself is the way to understand, through inquiry, one's true nature."

Commentary: Sri Bhagavan's approach to the revelation of the sublime truth of Advaita is to immediately direct the seeker to know the "I." Because of ignorance regarding the "I," illusion and "samsara" appear. If there be true knowledge of "I," illusion and samsara disappear...

Quite obviously, Nome writes not from book knowledge but from experience. This is so from question one to question forty. There is no false note, no wavering of understanding.

One cannot but be grateful to Nome for opening our eyes to many rare gems embedded in this work of Ramana, which is somewhat neglected. I am thankful to Nome for giving me an opportunity of writing a Foreword to this spiritual treasure.

~A.R. Natarajan
Ramana Maharshi Centre for Learning, Bangalore

INTRODUCTION

Obeisance to the perfect Guru, Bhagavan Sri Ramana Maharshi, who has revealed the Truth of the Self in flawless instruction and eloquent Silence, and who abides as That— Brahman. He is doubtlessly Siva, destroying the illusion of bondage. He reveals Self-Knowledge, perfect and true. To absorb his teaching, practice it, and realize it is to abide in eternal peace and illimitable bliss.

Abiding as the Self, he reveals the Self to the Self within the disciple. He eliminates the delusion of dualism and reveals the Self as the sole-existent Reality. It is indivisible Being-Consciousness. It is of the nature of infinite Wisdom and Bliss. For his grace and precious upadesa (spiritual instruction), we can never be too thankful.

What follows herein is a sacred scripture, for a scripture represents a direct revelation of the Truth free of mental conceptions. Bhagavan's teaching, when placed in printed words, is certainly scripture, for its significance is Truth transcending the words or thoughts utilized for its expression. This scripture is entitled *Vicharasangraham, The Compendium of Inquiry,* or, as it is generally known in English, *Self-Inquiry.* It has its origins in slips of paper upon which the Maharshi wrote answers to questions put to him by Gambhiram Seshayya during 1900 through 1902, when Sri Ramana was dwelling in Virupaksa Cave on holy Arunachala. Gambhiram Seshayya collected these slips and copied their contents into a notebook. It appears that he recorded both his questions and the answers, but, as the original slips of paper and the notebook are lost, it is not now possible to verify this with any certitude. It was many years later that these recordings were edited into a book by Sadhu Natanananda, and it was this that formed the published edition of the book, *Self-Inquiry.* In the course of time, different versions of this work in different languages, some in the original question-and-answer format and some in an essay form created by Sadhu Natanananda in the late 1930's, appeared. For this present publication, the original version translated into English, in question-and-answer format, which appears in the 1968 Indian edition of *The Collected Works of Ramana Maharshi,* edited by Author Osborne, has been selected. The English translation of the text is by the venerable T.M.P. Mahadevan. The well-researched articles regarding the various editions of *Self-Inquiry* that appeared in *The Mountain Path,* the journal of Sri Ramanasramam, Vol. 19, No.'s 1 and 2, January and April 1982 have also been consulted.

A careful reading of *Self-Inquiry* reveals that the teachings presented represent a display of his wondrous wisdom and compassion in many modes. Some statements are his direct declarations of the Truth. Some statements are commentary upon, or interpretation of, various spiritual texts. Some of his statements are made, in great compassion, in order to give that specific devotee, Gambhiram Seshayya, some means of grasping the teaching when the latter insisted on retaining opinions and views that are not based on the Knowledge of the Truth of the Self revealed by the Maharshi and Advaita Vedanta. Moreover, it would appear that Seshayya brought several scriptural texts to the Maharshi for him to comment upon or which were not comprehensible to that devotee. That Seshayya had an interest in Swami Vivekananda's *Raja Yoga* is mentioned in several articles and books about him and this text. A careful examination, though, of *Timeless in Time* and *Inner Circle,* both by A. R. Natarajan, and *Sri Ramana Leela,* by Sri Krishna Bhikshu and Pingali Surya Sundaram, reveals that it is Sadhu Natanananda who maintained from his youth a strong interest in Sri Ramakrishna and Swami Vivekananda, and this enduring interest can be seen very clearly in Sadhu Natanananda's own book, *Ramana Darsanam,* which he brought out in 1957. The above-mentioned *Mountain Path* articles state that, in his editorial work, Sadhu Natanananda not only deleted and arranged but also inserted what appears to be that which was of his own interest. Moreover, the Maharshi's comments on teachings of those contemporary with him are rather rare in all the recordings of the Maharshi's teachings, for evident spiritual reasons, but his profound, clarifying comments on scriptures such as the Upanishads

and the compositions of Adi Sankara, as well as other ancient works of time-honored sages and saints, are plentiful.
Self-Inquiry seems to employ the use of these other texts by
Sri Bhagavan extensively, most notably *Ribhu Gita, Yoga
Vasishtha,* and Adi Sankara's *Vivekacudamani.* This last
title is perhaps cited the most in *Self-Inquiry* and, along with
the other two, represents the earliest texts read by the Maharshi that corroborated his Self-Realization, which was attained spontaneously without recourse to any books
whatsoever. *Self-Inquiry* also references *Bhagavad Gita,
Skandopanishad, Mandukyopanishad,* and, it would seem,
a few other Upanishads. The *Mountain Path* articles previously mentioned also cite *Rama Gita* and *Brahma Gita* in
this respect, as well as point out that the picture-diagram is
derived from a description contained in the Tamil version of
Vedantachudamani. Sri Bhagavan, the Master of blissful
Wisdom, weaves the explanations of these scriptures with
his own words to reveal the eternal Truth—the Knowledge
of the Self. Thus, what correlation, if any, there may be of
the questions and answers contained in *Self-Inquiry* to contemporary teachings is unclear, be this in consideration of
the actual questions posed by the disciple and the answers
given by the Maharshi, the original notebook, or what appears in the later published editions. It is exceedingly clear,
though, through explanations of the teachings of the ancient
sages and his own spiritual instructions, that the Maharshi
herein reveals the timeless Truth of the Self and the direct
path of Self-inquiry that yields Self-Realization.

As the immutable Reality of the Self ever is and ever is
as it is, and as the Realization of the Self, being nondual, is
necessarily of the same nature as the Self, itself, there is a
perfect consistency in the teachings of Sri Bhagavan. Therefore, that which is revealed in this earliest recording of the
Maharshi's teachings is of identical meaning as that which
is found in *Who am I?*, the instructions of which were
recorded shortly thereafter, and that which is found in *Truth
Revealed (The Forty Verses on Reality),* which was composed
during a later period. Similarly, the teachings contained in
Talks with Sri Ramana Maharshi, Day by Day with Bhaga-

van, and many other works express the same supreme Truth and the same revelation of the inquiry that reveals it.

The commentary included herein is intended as auxiliary only for those who might find such of spiritual benefit. It is not intended to be representative of any scholarly erudition or to be exhaustive in its research of the scriptural references that abound in *Self-Inquiry.* One copy of the commentary was preserved in America by Sasvati, and another copy was also with Sri A. R. Natarajan in Bangalore at the Ramana Maharshi Centre for Learning, for about ten years. After that time, Sri Natarajan, who readily comprehended how such a book may serve a spiritual purpose, took it upon himself to publish what has now become the present book. The word of the Maharshi is the essence, and that, too, is rooted in His absolute Silence.

Words and phrases appearing within parenthesis in the actual text are those of the text itself as translated by T. M. P. Mahadevan and do not represent insertions by the commentator. Words appearing in brackets in other cited works that are mentioned in the commentary are insertions for the purpose of rendering the translation more readable. Except when otherwise indicated, translations within the commentary are from Sri A. R. Natarajan in publications of the Ramana Maharshi Centre for Learning, from publications of Sri Ramanasramam, from publications of the Society of Abidance in Truth, or by the author of the commentary.

One who approaches this sacred scripture with deep devotion and a sincere desire to realize the Self, and who, blessed by his grace, practices in accordance with the wisdom herein elucidated, will doubtlessly realize the sole-existent Self, the nondual Brahman, and abide as That, of the nature of undifferentiated Being-Consciousness-Bliss.

May Sri Bhagavan, my ever-gracious Guru, who is the Self that dwells in the hearts of all, be pleased with what is written here. May all be ever happy in the Realization of the Self.

ACKNOWLEDGEMENTS

Deep appreciation and gratitude are here expressed for Raman Muthukrishnan and Sangeeta Raman for proofreading this book and distribution of SAT publications, for Raymond Teague and Ganesh Sadasivan for proofreading, for Sasvati for design, layout and seeing to the printing, for Richard Schneider, Laura Pace, and all the SAT Temple devotees whose support of the temple and the publication of these teachings of Self-Knowledge has made the present book possible.

SAT wishes to also express its deep gratitude to Sri Ramanasramam for kindly granting permission to SAT to publish this present book.

SELF-INQUIRY
(VICHARASANGRAHAM)

Commentary: The revelation of Truth truly begins with Silence. This Silence is of the nature of the undifferentiated Reality, the nondual Truth. This sacred Silence of Sri Bhagavan is eternal. In this Silence, there is no other. Silence is ineffable. The only adequate description of Silence is Silence itself. In this Silence, the entirety of what follows is.

Invocation: Is there any way of adoring the Supreme, which is all, except by abiding firmly as That!

1

Disciple: Master! What is the means to gain the state of eternal Bliss, ever devoid of misery?

The Maharshi: Apart from the statement in the Veda that wherever there is the body there is misery, this is also the direct experience of all people; therefore, one should inquire into one's true nature, which is ever bodiless, and one should remain as such. This is the means to gaining that state.

Commentary:

Om Namo Bhagavate Sri Ramanaya

The Absolute is, by its very nature, Bliss. All beings seek this profound happiness, yet only they who seek it in the Absolute find it. The various approaches to realizing the Absolute manifest as the myriad modes of worship. The essence of all modes of worship or adoration that result in Realization of the Absolute is the dissolution of the ego, which is but a figment of imagination. From and in the ego is all ignorance, and ignorance alone is the cause of suffering. Worship that destroys this illusory entity, ego, is true worship, or adoration. It yields Self-Knowledge, which is the state of unceasing Bliss.

That which is the Supreme is all in all at all times. Dualism is a product of delusion. Nonduality is the nature of reality. One Existence is; it is all-pervasive. There is neither you nor I, neither the world nor anyone to experience it, neither creation nor destruction—nothing whatsoever at any time. The Absolute, the one Self, alone exists eternally.

Sri Bhagavan declares that there is no other way of truly adoring, or worshipping, the Absolute, which is that one, nondual Being, except by firmly abiding as That. This is the highest explanation of spiritual practice and how such is undifferentiated from Realization itself. Spiritual practice is for the purpose of enabling one to abide in the egoless, natural state of the Self. In this egoless, natural state, the Self and the Absolute are realized as identical, for the Absolute is nonobjective, and the Self—Being—is not an individual entity. To worship without a trace of the ego is sublime. In such worship, none of the illusions and sufferings of the ego remain. The worshipper and the worshipped are directly experienced as one and the same. Abidance as That, firm, without the least trace of misidentification or dualism, is the supreme worship of the Supreme. Since the Supreme is all, how can the illusion of a separate entity continue? By the compassionate word of the Maharshi, by the pure Knowledge revealed by the Maharshi, and by the illimitable grace of the Maharshi, we know this to be the truth.

The earnest disciple, who aspires for Self-Realization, seeks liberation from samsara, the illusory cycle of birth, death, and repetitive suffering. Such a disciple, not feeling the immediate, uninterrupted, ever-existent presence of the Self, seeks that eternal Bliss. Wisely, he approaches the great Sage, the Maharshi. Sri Bhagavan is Being-Consciousness-Bliss, itself. He abides eternally as the Self. To receive any instruction from him is the most wondrous blessing. The presence of such a jnani is that of unalloyed, undecaying grace. To experience it in any manner whatsoever is the most blessed opportunity anyone could ever have. It heralds in the destruction of samsara, as the rising sun at dawn does the disappearance of darkness. For those thirsty for Knowledge and peace, he is the nectarean ocean of Truth and Bliss. For

2

those stricken with the disease of suffering and the fever of delusion, his very presence is the perfect remedy of permanent happiness and the cool, clear Knowledge of Reality. Such a guru as the Maharshi brings one from darkness to light, from the unreal to the Real, from death to immortality.

The Self is the perfect fullness of supreme Bliss. If ignorance regarding its nature prevails in one's experience, such ignorance, of the character of misidentification, results in the illusion of bondage, which is experienced as suffering. Therefore, to eliminate suffering, one should destroy the illusory, limiting fetters. To destroy such bondage, one should abandon the misidentification constituting ignorance. When such ignorance is abandoned, Self-Knowledge shines resplendently, and the Bliss of that abidance in Self-Knowledge is unconditional and unending. For the purpose of revealing this sublime Knowledge of the Self, the Maharshi bestows instruction regarding the inquiry to know the Self.

Why should one inquire? It is to realize the Self as it is. What is the motivation for inquiring? It is the desire for happiness, which is the intuition of the nature of the Self. Thus, in Sri Bhagavan's teachings expressed in *Who am I?*, "Every living being longs always to be happy untainted by sorrow; and everyone has the greatest love for himself, which is solely due to the fact that happiness is his real nature. Hence, in order to realize that inherent nature and untainted happiness, which, indeed, he daily experiences when the mind is subdued in deep sleep, it is essential that he should know himself. For obtaining such knowledge, the inquiry, 'Who am I?' in quest of the Self is the means par excellence." As Being is Bliss, there is no other way to abide in happiness than Realization of the Self. Just as the desire for happiness cannot be stopped, but can be fulfilled only in this way, so the inquiry does not cease but is completed only in that nondual Realization.

The Maharshi says that the misidentification with the body—the illusion of its existence and the ignorance of conceiving it as one's identity—is, indeed, the cause of misery. This is revealed in the ancient scriptures, the Vedas, as well, which, especially in the Upanishads, contain the sacred

3

teachings of ancient sages. The wisdom contained therein is read or heard, reflected upon, and profoundly meditated upon, until it is realized by those who desire to know the timeless Truth. Such ancient teaching, as with that of Sri Bhagavan, is a description of experience, both in its explanation of the suffering of illusion and in its revelation of the reality of the Self. One has only to abandon the sankalpa-s (notions assumed to be valid due simply to lack of inquiry) in order to recognize the irrefutable truth revealed by the Maharshi and by other sages who, throughout time, expounded this pure Advaita Vedanta.

To equate the Self with the body is ignorance and misery. To know the true nature of the Self to be bodiless is blissful Self-knowledge. Compare and contrast the changeful, sporadic, limited, objective, dependent, indirectly known, transitory character of the body with the immutable, continuous, unlimited, nonobjective, nondependent, directly known, eternal nature of the Self, and you realize how the Self is not the body. The Self is not the body, nor in a body, nor in possession of a body. The Self's nature is forever infinite and formless. It is bodiless Being-Consciousness-Bliss. To be as you are is the purpose of spiritual practice. Abidance as you are, as forever unmodified Being, is Realization and Bliss. The inquiry, proclaims Sri Ramana Maharshi, the glorious guru, is the means of attaining that state, while the state, itself, is sahaja—natural, innate, and effortless— and truly has no alternative. Therefore, in *Who am I?*, (eighth edition, 1955) the Maharshi says, "That which is Bliss is, verily, the Self. Bliss and the Self are not distinct and separate, but are one and identical. And that alone is Real."

May all deeply meditate upon the Truth revealed by the Maharshi and, abiding in his grace and in that Truth revealed, dwell in perpetual Bliss and Peace. Whoever deeply inquires as instructed by the Maharshi realizes the true nature of the Self to be ever bodiless and, liberated from bondage and its consequent suffering, abides in infinite Wisdom and Bliss.

Om Sri Ramanarpanamastu
Om May this be an offering to Sri Ramana

2

Disciple: What is meant by saying that one should inquire into one's true nature and understand it?

The Maharshi: Experiences such as "I went; I came; I was; I did" come naturally to everyone. From these experiences, does it not appear that the consciousness "I" is the subject of those various acts? Inquiring into the true nature of that consciousness and remaining as oneself is the way to understand, through inquiry, one's true nature.

Commentary:

Om Namo Bhagavate Sri Ramanaya

Sri Bhagavan's approach to the revelation of the sublime Truth of Advaita Vedanta is to immediately direct the seeker to know the "I." Because of ignorance regarding the "I," illusion and samsara appear. If there be true Knowledge of the "I," illusion and samsara disappear. What remains is the blissful Self, the Reality of nondual Being.

For the seeker of Self-Realization, the Maharshi, as sadguru, gives the "push from without" and the "pull from within," revealing the direct path and the nature of the Self. To be touched by his grace and to be awakened by his illuminative Knowledge is a great blessing indeed. Fortunate are they who have such a guru!

The Maharshi always emphasizes the importance of Self-inquiry and Self-Knowledge. Knowledge of the Self is direct experience of the Self. This Knowledge transcends all words and thoughts; this direct experience is free of dualisms such as "subject-and-object" and is of an eternal nature. In order to realize the Self, that is, to abide in Self-Knowledge, one should inquire to know oneself. Therefore, the disciple asks to know the true significance of the inquiry and the real meaning of "understanding" one's true nature.

The body is naturally subject to change and motion. It engages in action. It is a fleeting appearance in time. Commonly, people say or think, "I went," "I came," "I was"— when recounting the past—"I did," and so forth and so on. Yet, Sri Bhagavan points out that the body and these attributes or activities of the body are of an objective, inert character, and there is an "I" that knows all these experiences. This knowing "I" is Consciousness. When unknown, it is mistaken for the body, misidentified with the senses, or assumed to be an individualized "consciousness" or mind. Upon reflection, one can clearly see that "I" am the knower, or subject, of all those various experiences and not the known, that is the body, and not related to the known, that is, the attributes and activities of the body. To the body belongs birth, apparent form, and death. The Self, though, being bodiless, is birthless, formless, and deathless.

Having determined that that which is objective cannot be the Self, one should inquire into the true nature of the "I," Consciousness, which is ever the knower, in order to realize the unalloyed, blissful Being that truly is the Self. The Maharshi declares that the inquiry that penetrates into our true nature—the nature of Consciousness, itself—is the way to "understand one's true nature," that is, to abide in Self-Knowledge, which has been proclaimed by all sages of all times to be the supreme state. This inquiry should be conducted with full intensity, in a concentrated manner, and with a determined desire to know the Truth. If, having negated all that is objective, one remains unswervingly absorbed in the inquiry into one's true nature, the Self is revealed. That Self is Being-Consciousness-Bliss. To be as you are is the state of Self-Knowledge. It is not knowing "this" or "that." The Self's being as it is, unobscured by any notion, be it of "I" or the "body," is the natural state of Self-Realization. Liberating oneself from misidentifications and remaining as Being-Consciousness, free from the formation of misidentifications, is the essence of the inquiry. To "be as you are" should not be misinterpreted as remaining with the misidentification as a cognizing entity in space and time. Rather, this instruction by the Maharshi signifies abidance as Being without any ego or any misidentification.

If one practices the path revealed by Sri Bhagavan, the highest Realization results. By grace we know of him. By grace we understand. By grace we practice. By grace we realize.

Ever aware of this grace, let there be steadfast inquiry into the Self, and the real nature of the Self becomes self-evident. Whoever inquires into the true nature of Consciousness realizes his Being and, remaining as the Self, in Self-Knowledge, abides in infinite Wisdom and Bliss.

Om Sri Ramanarpanamastu
Om May this be an offering to Sri Ramana

3

Commentary:

Om Namo Bhagavate Sri Ramanaya

Transcendent of the body and the false notion of an individual "I," or ego, our sadguru, Sri Bhagavan, abides in the natural state of Self-Realization. The Maharshi, full of grace and Knowledge, abiding imperturbably in that state, bestows the wondrous Knowledge of the Self on his blessed disciples. Following the path elucidated by him, they inquire into the nature of the Self and are set free from the fetters of ignorance.

The Maharshi previously declared, "Inquiring into the true nature of that consciousness and remaining as oneself is the way to understand, through inquiry, one's true nature." Therefore, the disciple, in earnest to know how to realize the Self and thus abide in limitless bliss, asks,

Disciple: How is one to inquire, "Who am I?"

The Maharshi: Actions such as "going" and "coming" belong only to the body. And so, when one says, "I went, I came," it amounts to saying that the body is "I." But, can the body be said to be the consciousness "I," since the body was not before it was born, is made up of the five elements, is nonexistent in the state of deep sleep, and becomes a corpse when dead? Can this body, which is inert like a log of wood, be said to shine as "I"-"I"? Therefore, the "I" consciousness, which at first arises in respect of the body, is referred to variously as self-conceit (tarbodham), egoity (ahankara), nescience (avidya), maya, impurity (mala), and individual soul (jiva). Can we remain without inquiry into

7

this? Is it not for our redemption through inquiry that all the scriptures declare that the destruction of "self-conceit" is release (mukti)?

Commentary:
Consider the first half of Sri Bhagavan's profound answer, which is what is presented thus far. He commences by pointing out that all connection with oneself of activity, motion, doership, and similar notions and attributes, which refer to the body, is due to the misidentification of the Self with the body. Only the body is born, moves, appears to live and die, and undergoes all kinds of change. These do not belong to our real Being. By superimposition of the reality and identity of the Self upon the body, it is mistaken to be "I," and by the superimposition of the attributes of the body upon the Self, the Self is erroneously conceived as being endowed with qualities, actions, etc.

The consciousness or feeling of "I" derives from a deep source. Is that source the body? The body has a birth; the "I" for which the experience of the body arises exists prior to the birth of the body. The body is a composite of elements, or the five states of matter; the "I" is not composed of such inert elements. The body is an image of the waking state of mind—just as a dream body is an image of the dream state of mind—and does not exist in the deep sleep state, in which there is neither thought nor a body; the Self subsists throughout all three states and is never an object of perception or conception. As certain as there was birth of the body, so certain is the death of the body. The "I," which did not commence at birth, does not cease with the death of the body.

Since the Self is nonobjective and not to be newly attained, for it is ever present, the inquiry is primarily a negation of that which is not the Self. This negation of that which is not the Self is given similar expression by Sri Bhagavan in *Who am I?* as, "Who am I? I am not this physical body, nor am I the five organs of sense-perception; I am not the five organs of external activity, nor am I the five vital forces, nor am I even the thinking mind. Neither am I that unconscious state of nescience that retains merely the subtle vasana-s

8

(latencies of the mind), being then free from the functional activity of the sense-organs and of the mind, and being unaware of existence of the objects of sense perception. Therefore, summarily rejecting all the above-mentioned physical adjuncts and their functions, saying, 'I am not this, no, nor am I this, nor this,' that which then remains separate and alone by itself, that pure Awareness, verily, am I. This Awareness is, by its very nature, Sat-Chit-Ananda (Existence-Consciousness-Bliss)." Thus, the misidentifications are negated, which means that one's identity is no longer mixed up with that which is not truly the Self. The freedom from misidentification with the body is pivotal for fruitful inquiry, which results in liberation from the ego, the source of all other delusion.

The body is merely an illusory, objective appearance. The "I" derives from a continuously present Existence, of the nature of unalloyed Consciousness. This Being-Consciousness is truly the Self. It is referred to by the Maharshi and by the rishi Ribhu as "I"-"I." It is formless, nondual, self-luminous, ever present, and bodiless.

The "I"—a second to the real Self—that rises and disappears and that is defined as a body or as in a body or as endowed with a body is the ego. It is individualized and, in delusion, considers this individuality to be real and vital. It is the source of ignorance and is nescience itself, containing all forms of delusion within itself. It is the only "impurity"— this delusion of a jiva in the midst of the omnipresent, homogeneous, undifferentiated, infinite, space-like Brahman. It is maya—illusion. Illusion is that which is not.

If the ego is destroyed, one's direct experience is that of the blissful Self. As the ego is only nescience, Knowledge alone destroys it. To attain this Knowledge, one should inquire as to "Who am I?" This inquiry, pursued with intensity, with perseverance, and with the earnest desire to realize the Self, is the means by which our own real Being, egoless and bodiless, becomes self-revealed.

The Vedanta scriptures declare that the destruction of the illusory ego is Mukti, Liberation. It is release from all of the imagined bondage. It is the perfect peace and boundless freedom of our natural state. It is Self-Knowledge. It is the one state of the Self and has no alternative.

To remain without inquiring as the Maharshi reveals is to wallow in the quagmire of the ego's delusion. Once one has recognized the Self as being Bliss itself—and the illusory ego as alone the veil concealing it—who would not inquire and thus realize the Self?

Being the recipient of such Grace, and aware of the indisputable validity of Sri Bhagavan's supreme wisdom, dive within by inquiry and thus know yourself, in infinite Wisdom and Bliss. Whoever so inquires destroys the misidentification with the body and the falsely assumed ego and, as proclaimed by countless scriptural texts, abides in infinite Wisdom and Bliss.

Om Sri Ramanarpanamastu
Om May this be an offering to Sri Ramana

3

(continued)

The Maharshi: Therefore, making the corpse-body remain as a corpse, and not even uttering the word "I," one should inquire keenly thus: "Now, what is it that rises as 'I'"? Then, there would shine in the Heart a kind of wordless illumination of the form "I" "I." That is, there would shine of its own accord the pure Consciousness, which is unlimited and one, the limited and the many thoughts having disappeared. If one remains quiescent without abandoning that (experience), the egoity, the individual sense, of the form "I am the body," will be totally destroyed, and, at the end, the final thought, viz., the "I"-form also will be quenched like the fire that burns camphor. The great sages and scriptures declare that this alone is release.

Commentary:

Om Namo Bhagavate Sri Ramanaya

The ever-gracious Maharshi continues his instruction concerning the true nature of the Self and the efficacy of Self-inquiry in attaining Self-Realization. Mukti, or Liberation, consists of freedom from misidentification with the body and destruction of the illusory ego. Thus, Liberation is freedom from imagined bondage, but the resultant Bliss is real. It is the Bliss of the Self.

In *Words of Grace,* which contains an essay form of *Self-Inquiry,* this same sublime instruction given by Sri Bhagavan is stated thus: "Therefore, lay aside this insentient body as though it were truly a corpse. Do not even murmur "I," but inquire keenly within what it is that now shines within the heart as "I." Underlying the unceasing flow of varied thoughts, there arises the continuous, unbroken awareness, silent and spontaneous, as "I"-"I" in the Heart. If one catches hold of it and remains still, it will completely annihilate the sense of "I" in the body, and it will itself disappear as does a fire of burning camphor. Sages and scriptures proclaim this to be Liberation."

The prime form of misidentification is the superimposition of one's identity upon the body. To regard the body as the Self is ignorance. To know that the Self is not the body is the dawn of Self-Knowledge and is essential for the destruction of the illusory ego. The Maharshi says that we should regard the body as no more than a corpse, an insentient object that cannot at all be equated with the Consciousness that is our true Being.

Without misidentifying the "I" with the body, without an "I" being the center of one's speech or mind, one must inquire into this sense of "I." It appears as if individualized—and such is called delusion—but, in truth, that which shines within the Heart, the very essence of our Being, is the unlimited Self. That Self is silent, natural, formless, immutable, continuous, and self-effulgent. It is Consciousness, the uncreated substratum beneath the flow of thoughts. Those thoughts may be divine, but this Consciousness is nondual. In truth, Consciousness alone is, and thought is nonexistent. Consciousness perceived through delusion appears as thought. When one inquires into the nature of the Self, Consciousness, itself, is directly known free from thought. The Self ever is as it is and never becomes thought. Thought has no existence but Consciousness, yet Consciousness never becomes thought. The Realization of the ever-present, nondual Consciousness constitutes freedom from thought.

It is in thought that limitation and bondage are imagined. Transcendent of thought, true Being has no bondage whatsoever.

To remain quiescent in the Self without imagining the ego "I" and its embodiment is to be at peace, awake to the Reality. By constantly inquiring as to "Who am I?" the ego, the I-am-the-body notion, and all illusion vanish. Even the "I"-sense, as a "feeling" or as individualized in any way, vanishes by such profound inquiry, just as when camphor is set ablaze not a trace of it remains. Indeed, the fragrance is most noticeable at the moment it extinguishes itself when there is no more camphor to act as fuel; similarly the vasana-s and the very notion of "I" are burned entirely by the inquiry, and upon their utter extinguishment in Brahman (Brahma-nirvana), (the Self), the sweet fragrance of Bliss is all-pervasive.

The blissful state of abidance as the Self is liberation, or release, from birth, death, and all suffering. It is the essential message of the scriptures. It is the state of all sages such as the Maharshi.

Sri Bhagavan, abiding as the one Self, which alone exists eternally, reveals the truth regarding the Self. With infinite Grace and boundless compassion, he has revealed the way to realize this ever-present Self. He makes flawlessly clear the essence of Vedanta, the Knowledge of the Absolute.

If one can only realize at Heart the Truth he has revealed—the Truth of the Self—one will find it is infinite Wisdom and Bliss.

Sri Bhagavan has already thoroughly, clearly revealed that the Self is not the body. To confound the Self with the body is ignorance. The release of such misidentification brings Self-Knowledge and liberation from bondage.

The Self is of the nature of Being-Consciousness-Bliss. It has neither birth nor death, is immutable and ever present, and abides free of form. This is who we are, our real Existence. The body is only an illusion of transitory, objective form. It is dead form; the Self is the essence—immortal Being. The inquiry into the true nature of the Self does not newly make the Self unembodied or newly make the body to be other than the Self. The Self is innately bodiless, and one has only to see that this is true and remain in such Knowledge rather than returning to the delusion of misidentification. Abide in the liberating Knowledge that the body is not the Self; this is making the corpse-body remain as a corpse.

The inquiry revealed by the Maharshi requires an intense, undistracted, inward focus unimpeded by vasana-s (tendencies). One must be without the misidentification with the particular thoughts that constitute the personality. One must be free of every attribute, quality, action, etc., predicated of the ego "I" and keenly inquire to know what it is that appears as "I." The individual (ego) "I" thus proves to be absent, there truly being nothing that answers to the name of "I." What was mistakenly assumed to be an individual "I" is actually the nondual, indivisible, absolute Being of the Self. When the inquiry is made, the superimposition of this false individuality upon one's real Existence and the projection of the reality of Being upon that false assumption cease. What remains in the Heart—one's quintessential Being—is the "wordless illumination" of "I-I." "I-I," a term used by the Maharshi and by Ribhu, refers to the Self, being itself, which is knowing itself. The Self is Consciousness, transcendent of all definition and of all words and thought.

Consciousness is Being. As Being ever is, Consciousness always is. If form or multiplicity appears, it is only Consciousness that shines so that such can be seen. It is the one knower of all that is known. It shines upon itself, for it is all in all at all times. The Realization of the Self is simply the extinguishment of ignorance. It does not cause Consciousness to begin to shine. It has been, is, and will be shining for all eternity. It is eternal, and it is infinite. Limitations are only false notions. With the disappearance of notions, limitations vanish, and the Self, of the nature of unalloyed Consciousness, remains, self-effulgent, nondual, and ever free.

Once you have entered the Knowledge of the Self, do not abandon that great source of Bliss. Remain quiescent, and do not conjure up more delusions of an "I" and "I-am-the-body." If such ignorance arises, inquire to free yourself

of the misidentification with the body and every other notion. Persist so that the destruction of illusion is complete
and abidance in the Self is steady. When the final notion,
that is the "I"-notion, is abandoned, there is then no further
effort. With the disappearance of the "I," the very possibility
of illusion, ignorance, and samsara is gone. When the fuel of
camphor is gone, the flame extinguishes itself; only the fragrance in empty space remains. Meditating upon the true
nature of the "I," all the fuel of vasana-s, sankalpa-s, notions,
etc., is burned up in inquiry's conflagration; the fuel gone,
the "I"—and the inquiry into it—is extinguished. What remains is the sweet fragrance of Bliss pervading the infinity
of space-like Being.

This is release from all fetters, Liberation from all the
imagined bondage. This Realization is the purpose and revelation of the nondual scriptures and the teaching of all Self-
Realized sages. The Maharshi is such a great sage
(Maha-rishi, great rishi). His teaching is sublime, his grace
supreme. The complete realization of just one line—even one
phrase or word—or his Silence bestows highest Knowledge
and endless peace. To feel his presence in your heart is to be
fulfilled. To have his darshan is to have the darshan of Siva,
himself. To be with him is to be with Brahman, itself. To follow his instruction is to awaken to Reality. With Sri Bhagavan as Sadguru, there is absorption in infinite Wisdom,
Truth, and Bliss alone.

Whoever inquires to know the "I" in its real nature realizes the self-luminous pure Consciousness of the Self,
which is limitless and nondual, and ever abiding as That,
dwells in infinite Wisdom and Bliss.

Om Sri Ramanarpanamastu
Om May this be an offering to Sri Ramana

4

Disciple: When one inquires into the root of "self-conceit," which is of the form "I," all sorts of different thoughts
without number seem to rise and not any separate "I"
thought.

The Maharshi: Whether the nominative case, which is the first case, appears or not, the sentences in which the other cases appear have as their basis the first case; similarly, all the thoughts that appear in the heart have as their basis the egoity, which is the first mental mode "I," the cognition of the form "I am the body"; thus, it is the rise of egoity that is the cause and source of the rise of all other thoughts; therefore, if the self-conceit of the form of egoity, which is the root of the illusory tree of samsara (bondage consisting of transmigration), is destroyed, all other thoughts will perish completely like an uprooted tree.

Commentary:
Om Namo Bhagavate Sri Ramanaya

The web of illusion is spun by thought. The dream of samsara, the repetitive cycle of illusory birth and death, is a conjuration of thought. Gracious Sadguru Ramana destroys this ephemeral, illusory dream of bondage by revealing the truth of the Self. If the Self is known, ignorance vanishes, and all trace of bondage disappears.

The disciple yearns to trace the root of "self-conceit," the collection of notions that preposterously declare differentiation in the midst of formless Being, that claim individual selfhood in the midst of infinite Consciousness, that claim importance of the jiva when only Siva—Brahman—is real. He perceives that there must be a root to this self-conceit and that such a root must be of the form of "I." Yet, searching for an "I"-thought, he perceives ever so many ideas but not the actual thought "I."

The Maharshi, full of compassion and wisdom, reveals a deeper view of the inquiry into the "I" to find the Self. Whether one observes a particular thought "I" or not, the subtle notion or assumption of the "I's" existence is present. The assumption of a separate "I," or ego, is the foundation for all delusion and samsara.

The Heart is vast and space-like. The first imagined difference is that of a separate "I." The "I" still has no form of its own; the body becomes the form with which it misidentifies. None of this occurs outside the Heart. The Heart is the Self. The Self is neither an "I" nor a body.

Without the "I," there can be no other notion. With no ego, there is nothing objective. Without body misidentification, there are no births and deaths.

Therefore, to be free of the bondage by thoughts, one should inquire into their root and basis—the "I." Inquire and know the Self, and you realize the nonexistence of the ego and all that is based upon it. The one Self alone exists.

What is declared here in *Self-Inquiry* by the Maharshi is very similar to the instruction of his contained in *Who am I?*: "The first and foremost of all the thoughts that arise in the mind is the primal 'I'-thought. It is only after the rise or origin of the 'I'-thought that innumerable other thoughts arise. In other words, only after the first personal pronoun, 'I,' has arisen, do the second and third personal pronouns (you, he, etc.) occur to the mind; and they cannot subsist without the former. Since every other thought can occur only after the rise of the 'I'-thought, and since the mind is nothing but a bundle of thoughts, it is only through the inquiry, 'Who am I?' that the mind subsides. Moreover, the integral 'I'-thought, implied in such inquiry, having destroyed all other thoughts, gets itself finally destroyed or consumed, even like the stick used for stirring the burning funeral pyre gets consumed." Similarly, in *Saddarshanam*, verse 14 (Sri A. R. Natarajan's translation), the Maharshi proclaims, "Without the 'I,' the second and third persons cannot exist; when the 'I' subsides through inquiry about its source, the second and third persons, too, disappear. Our own natural state shines forth."

All the other notions that follow upon the ego notion, or "I"-mode (aham vritti), are only for that "I," and not truly for the Self, which abides without a second. They are rooted in the "I," which is, itself, as an illusion, rootless, and as a misperception of that which is actually existent, the undivided Reality of the Self. They are entirely that notion of "I," the assumption of existing as an individual entity, in various guises. They do not exist apart from that "I." Therefore, by questioning for whom these thoughts appear, the reality and identity are traced inward to the "I" and by inquiring, "Who am I?", both the delusive ego-"I" and all its permutations in the form of the various thoughts are found not to exist. This Knowledge is, therefore, complete destruction. Such destruction cannot be a mental state, whether with thought activity or without, but, to be eternal and innate, must be mind-transcendent. That is Self-Knowledge, in which neither the ego nor its imagined creations exist. From that which does not exist, no bondage can come. This is Liberation. For one who has never been born, there can be no cycle of transmigration. The Realization of no ego is said to be its (the ego's, illusion's) destruction. In that in which there is no ego, no samsara can be. How else is one to realize this Truth of the Self except by the profound inquiry to know the Self? By the grace of the One who is himself that Self, the guru who liberates all those who, struggling in samsara, adhere to his Self-revealing teachings, the Maharshi, it is so.

By following the direct path revealed by Sri Bhagavan, one is liberated from all the imagined bondage and dwells in peace and happiness. Abidance as the Self is the nondual, supreme state. If one can only realize at Heart the Truth he has revealed, one will find that this is the natural state of infinite Wisdom and Bliss.

Om Sri Ramanarpanamastu

Om May this be an offering to Sri Ramana

4

(continued)

The Maharshi: Whatever thoughts arise as obstacles to one's sadhana—the mind should not be allowed to go in their direction, but should be made to rest in one's Self, which is the Atman; one should remain as the witness to whatever happens, adopting the attitude, "Let whatever strange things happen, happen; let us see!" This should be one's practice. In other words, one should not identify oneself with appearances; one should never relinquish one's Self.

Commentary:

Om Namo Bhagavate Sri Ramanaya

The purpose of sadhana is the attainment of Self-Realization. Self-Realization is not the attainment of something other than that which is ever-existent—pure Being. Being ever is, formless, quiescent, birthless, deathless, innately perfectly full, and of uncaused, unlimited bliss. Self-Realization is abidance as the Self, which one ever is. It is to be as you are. Therefore, in essence, the purpose of sadhana is to cause you to be as you are. Yet, since the Self is always present, sadhana consists in the removal of obscuring ignorance, which seems to veil the Self's own nature from one's own view.

Ignorance alone represents the obstacles to sadhana and Realization. Ignorance is insubstantial, being composed of mere imagination manifesting as sankalpa-s—ideas or thoughts assumed to be real and valid due only to lack of clear inquiry. When carefully scrutinized, the obstacles to one's sadhana prove to be nothing other than one's own thoughts. The inert, unreal world, body, etc., are not obstacles. Moreover, they appear only in the mind and have no existence apart from the thought of them.

Two aspects of thought's obstruction should be recognized and transcended by one who seeks to realize the Self and thus abide in perpetual bliss and Liberation. First, one must recognize all suffering-and-bondage-producing vasana-s (tendencies) and, through the power of nonattachment and inquiry, destroy them. Nonattachment derives from the knowledge of the source of happiness, which is within. Inquiry is the experiential determination of what, in truth, is one's identity. The second aspect involves the supposition of thought's existence. Thoughts are not self-existent, but are always in relation to the "I" which knows them. If, as revealed by the ever-gracious sage of steady, supreme Wisdom—Sri Bhagavan—the inquiry is made as "For whom are these thoughts?" the sense of "reality" and "identity" will return to the "I," and the objective unreality, namely thought, inclusive of all its content, will be realized to be nonexistent. If one continues the inquiry as to "Who am I?"

the Self will assuredly be realized. It is that which alone is, the nondual absolute Reality, Brahman. Hence, one should release oneself from the thoughts that arise as obstacles, that is, the thoughts of bondage and the notion that thought is existent.

Thus, in order to accomplish this the Maharshi gives the instruction that the mind should not be allowed to go in the direction of obscuring ideas but should be made to rest in one's Self, which is the Atman. If the mind is made to fall in the direction of obscuring concepts, which are but imagined within itself, the illusion appears as if the mind is a separate entity, bound, obstructed, thwarted, and made miserable by these thoughts, which are viewed as other, objectively existing entities creating a labyrinthine prison for itself. Such involves the superimposition of thoughts on Consciousness, or we may say the projection of knowing, which belongs to Consciousness alone, upon thought so that the mind appears as if it were a knowing entity. With repetition, such thoughts become vasana-s; when the reality of Being is projected on them, they appear as if an externalized world; and, with the projection of Bliss upon them, they manifest as vain attachments to the things of that unreal world. The wise do not place their minds in this direction.

The wise turn their minds within, dissolving the superimpositions and destroying all those illusions. When the mind turns within, it is liberated from its self-created bondage. Turning within, it loses its form. Within, it is absorbed in oneself. The Maharshi declares the truth that one's self is the Self, the Atman, and not anything else. That Atman, declared by the sages to be immortal, unborn, qualitiless, immutable, eternal, infinite, all transcendent, Brahman itself, Siva Himself, is yourself. That Self is ineffable and inconceivable; only a wondrous guru like Sri Ramana can reveal the Truth of the Self.

The Maharshi then reveals what it means to be the detached witness. What is the witness? It is none other than the Self, of the nature of unalloyed Consciousness. This Consciousness is, in reality, uncreated, indescribable, partless, and devoid of the triad of knower, knowing, and known.

When considered in relation to anything else—thoughts or sense perceptions—it is the witness. The witness is silent and serene, shining timelessly, forever free, and never an object of perception or conception. It is ever unaffected by all thought and all states of mind. It is not a mentally developed perspective. Rather, it is the continuously present, nonobjective knower of all that is known. To abide as the witness is natural. It is to be free of misidentification and attachments. For one who is firmly established as Consciousness, the witness of all, the appearance and disappearance of the universe and of thought make no difference whatsoever. No-creation is the natural state. It is the undifferentiated Reality. The wise, abiding in That, as the blissful witness, view the wondrous, false occurrences of the appearance and disappearance of anything in a manner of complete detachment. If one practices in this light, identifying only with the witness and remaining nonattached to all else, all fears and desires vanish, and the sublime Truth of the Self will be realized.

To attain Self-Knowledge, do not misidentify with appearances, which are characterized by mutability, transience, duality, form, and objectivity. Steadily hold to the Self as it is, and you will awaken to the Truth that you are That.

May all who are so blessed to receive the sacred teaching of Sri Bhagavan, shining as the quintessential Advaita Vedanta, follow his profound instruction in every detail. They will thus realize the Self and abide in infinite Wisdom and Bliss.

Om Sri Ramanarpanamastu

Om May this be an offering to Sri Ramana

4

(continued)

The Maharshi: This is the proper means for destruction of the mind (manonasa), which is of the nature of seeing the body as the Self and which is the cause of all the aforesaid obstacles. This method, which easily destroys egoity, deserves to be called devotion (bhakti), meditation (dhyana), concentration (yoga), and knowledge (jnana). Because God remains of the nature of the Self, shining as "I" in the heart, because the scriptures declare that thought itself is bondage, the best discipline is to stay quiescent without ever forgetting Him (God, the Self), after resolving in Him the mind, which is of the form of the "I-thought," no matter by what means. This is the conclusive teaching of the scriptures.

Commentary:

Om Namo Bhagavate Sri Ramanaya

The true nature of the Self is pure Being-Consciousness-Bliss. The Self is formless, indivisible, and nondual. It ever is as it is. It is the one Reality. Sri Bhagavan's teaching is a continuous, flawless, completely enlightening revelation of the Self, the sole-existent Reality.

When the reality of pure Consciousness, which is the Self, is projected on the imagination of "existent thought," the result is the erroneous belief in an existent mind. The Maharshi has declared that the illusory knot tied between the Self and the body is the mind. In order for the mind to appear, it must have some form to grasp and with which to misidentify. That form is the body. The mind conceives a form within itself, posits the notion of an outside realm, projects its own notion into that realm (manifestation), imagines itself as if encased within its own notion (embodiment), and falsely declares its identity to be that notion (the body) while claiming to be, itself, the Self. Such is delusion. If the misidentification with the body is destroyed, one abides in the Self as the Self.

The mind is declared to be the cause of obstacles. What are these obstacles? They are the notions that obstruct one's sadhana. In other words, they are the obscuring ignorance that veils the nature of one's own Self and makes one believe himself to be other than the Self, as previously revealed.

If the mind is destroyed, the reality of pure, blissful Consciousness, unobscured and unobstructed, remains. The destruction of the mind is the cessation of dualism. The destruction of the mind is the obliteration of vasana-s and the impediments to unending peace. The destruction of the mind is the undoing of birth and the extinction of death. The destruction of the mind is the eradication of the causes of suffering. The destruction of the mind is the annihilation of fear. The destruction of the mind is the removal of ignorance. The destruction of the mind is the awakening from the dream-like illusion. The destruction of the mind is the destruction of the unreal.

Sri Bhagavan proclaims, "This is the proper means for destruction of the mind." What is the proper means? He has already revealed it: "One should not identify oneself with appearances; one should not relinquish one's Self." If there is no misidentification with appearances—anything objective, conceivable, mutable, subject to creation and destruction, in time and space, endowed with form, or other than the Self— one will abide in the Truth of the Self. If there is no conjuring up of misconceptions regarding one's nature and no return to the sankalpa-s or vasana-s, one does not relinquish this abidance in the Self. Such constitutes the destruction of the mind.

All false notions are based upon the primary false assumption of the ego, or "I"-notion. All bondage is nothing but the mind. The mind and its bondage are nothing but the ego. The destruction of the ego is the Realization of the Self. The destruction of the ego consists in the realization of its eternal absence.

Any method, under whatever name, that destroys the ego is conducive to the state of supreme Bliss. Whatever be the method practiced, if it dissolves the ego and causes one to no longer misidentify oneself with false appearances and to remain without relinquishing the Self, it is true and leads to the desired goal of Liberation. Indeed, it is just this that constitutes the essence of each path. So bhakti, or devotion, dissolves the ego, surrendering all so that nothing remains apart from the Supreme, which is God and which is Guru. The Guru, or God—the Supreme Self—alone remains, without a trace of separation. Dhyana, or meditation, eliminates the false notion of a meditator so that the triad of meditator, meditating, and the object of meditation vanishes. That upon which one meditates, the Absolute, is revealed as the Self and alone remains, without a trace of an alternative, non-meditative state. Yoga reveals the eternal union of oneself and the Absolute, dissolving the delusion of division. The Self alone remains, eternally, one-pointedly abiding in its own nature, the mind dissolved never to be recreated. Jnana is the Knowledge of Reality which is one without a second, which is utterly egoless, which is characterized by the absence of duality and of the triads, which never undergoes change or modification, which consists of Being reposing in itself as it is, which is the shining of the light of self-effulgent Consciousness upon itself. The Self alone remains, for it alone has always been and will be, and no trace of the illusory ignorance remains. Thus Sri Bhagavan has revealed the essence of all paths and practices.

Whatever be the means, the "I"-thought, or ego or mind, is resolved into That, be That called God or the Self. The unreal never comes to be. Thought of the unreal makes it appear real. In truth, thought itself is unreal. Thought alone appears as bondage. The truth regarding the Self is that it is ever free. To abide transcendent of all thought, with no false definitions superimposed on the real Self, is Liberation and is called "quiescence." This is also the never-forgetting of That. Such "remembrance" is not merely a thought form. It is continuous, inner Knowledge. It is the Knowledge of one's very Existence. We never forget that we are; thought to the contrary does not alter our existence. The true nature of this existence, transcendent of all thought and shining as the only "I" in the Heart—the quintessence of Being—is the Absolute. God is of the nature of the Self. God is not an objective thing, and the Self is not a separate individuality. This Self is Brahman, declare the Upanisads.

The Knowledge of the Self, of the indivisibility of the Self and Brahman, is the purport of the scriptures—the Upanisads as well as the many other texts intended for the instruction of those who seek the Realization of the Absolute. Indeed, a careful reading of chapters 15 and 36 of the Tamil *Ribhu Gita,* especially the former, will show mention of most, if not all, of the aspects of this wisdom so succinctly revealed here in the entirety of section four of *Self-Inquiry* by the Maharshi. It cannot now be determined if the Maharshi's words were spoken as a commentary upon those chapters of the *Ribhu Gita,* yet it can be determined, without a trace of doubt, that what he has taught is conclusive. This teaching is conclusive because it is the Truth. It is conclusive because it remains timelessly the same age after age, realized sage after realized sage. It is conclusive because, in it, the mind that might doubt it is nonexistent. It is conclusive for it is self-evident to the wise who see with the eye of Knowledge. It is conclusive because there exists no second thing (person) to refute it or conceive otherwise. It is conclusive because it is of the nature of direct experience.

Whoever perceives the preciousness and sublime nature of the Maharshi's teaching and knows it to be the eternal Truth and follows and practices it realizes the nondual Reality of the Self and abides in infinite Wisdom and Bliss.

Om Sri Ramanarpanamastu

Om May this be an offering to Sri Ramana

5

Disciple: Is inquiry only the means for removal of the false belief of selfhood in the gross body, or is it also the means for removal of the false belief of selfhood in the subtle and causal bodies?

The Maharshi: It is on the gross body that the other bodies subsist. In the false belief of the form "I am the body" are included all the three bodies consisting of the five sheaths. And destruction of the false belief of selfhood in the gross body is itself the destruction of the false belief of selfhood in the other bodies. So, inquiry is the means to removal of the false belief of selfhood in all the three bodies.

Commentary:

Om Namo Bhagavate Sri Ramanaya

In order to resolve all doubts and destroy all illusions, a disciple who is an earnest aspirant for Liberation approaches a Self-Realized guru to instruct him in the Truth. The guru, who abides in the natural state of perfect identity with the one Absolute, Brahman, liberates the disciple from all of the imagined bondage and enables the disciple to realize the Self, which is none other than Brahman. Fortunate, indeed, is this disciple who is blessed with the auspicious opportunity of approaching the Maharshi for instruction, for Sri Bhagavan is a sadguru of incomparable wisdom and illimitable grace.

It is fundamental for all who aspire to realize the Self to transcend the misidentification with the body. The gross, transitory, limited, objective, changeful body, subject to birth and death, is not the formless, eternal, infinite, nonobjective, immutable, unborn and undying Self. By the inquiry into the nature of the Self, one discerns by direct experience the Self's freedom from the body. One also realizes that there is no ego inhabiting the body. The ego is not an entity within the body, and the body does not produce an ego. By the inquiry into the Self, the misidentification with the body is destroyed, and the false belief in an existent ego is, similarly, destroyed.

The disciple wishes to know whether the inquiry liberates one from only the misidentification with the physical body, or whether it also removes the misidentification with the subtle and causal bodies. The gross is merely a manifestation of the subtle, which in turn, rises from the causal. To be entirely free of delusion, one must transcend all so that the very seeds of illusion are destroyed in the knowledge that reveals their nonexistence, and one abides as the immutable, illusion-less Self, the Reality, of the nature of Being-Consciousness-Bliss.

The triad of bodies consists of the five sheaths. The stula sarira, or gross body, consists of the annamaya kosa, or "sheath of food." It is composed of the five elements in fractional proportions. The sukshma sarira, or subtle body, consists of the pranamaya kosa, or sheath of prana (life energy or vital airs), the manomaya kosa, or sheath of the mind, and the vijnanamaya kosa, or sheath of intellect, intellectual knowledge, and relative awareness. The organs of actions are considered impelled by the prana, and the senses are considered under the control of the mind, or manomaya kosa. The karana sarira, or causal body, is composed of the anandamaya kosa, literally the sheath of bliss, and is of the nature of ignorance—but not the manifest forms of ignorance—that functions as the cause, or basis, of the other two bodies or four sheaths. Thus the bodies are the forms that the individual assumes. They are the forms of the experiencer, with the forms of experience always of a mirror-like character of those forms. Thus, if the form of the experiencer is causal, the experience will be of the form of the cause without any effect, in other words the darkness of the veil of ignorance without the effect of projected multiplicity, such as in deep sleep. If the form of the experiencer is subtle, the experience is subtle. If the form is physical, the world perceived from the physical body is the experience. It is evident that the experience of the gross depends upon the subtle, which depends upon the causal. Thus, all of these misidentifications are assumed by one who regards himself as the body.

Later, in *Saddarshanam*, (translation by Sri A. R. Natarajan) the Maharshi declared, "The body is made up of the five sheaths. The body and the world co-exist. Can anyone see the world unless he has a body?" Therefore, if the misidentification with body is eliminated, the world is also transcended, and, abandoning the five sheaths, one realizes the Self in its real nature.

The Self transcends all of these bodies or sheaths. Misidentification with these sheaths yields the illusion of a veil cast over the eternally present, self-effulgent Self. The very notion of the Self, of the nature of unalloyed, formless Consciousness, being endowed with a form is the significance of the "I-am-the-body" delusion. The ignorance present in misidentification with the bodily form (gross, physical) is the same that is present with misidentification with other forms, however subtle. The ignorance present in the "I-am-the-body" notion—the assumption of an existent, individual "I" endowed with or defined by a form—is the same constituting the "causal body." So, Sri Bhagavan declares that all such misidentification depends on the "I-am-the-body" notion, and the destruction of that false belief is the destruction of the misidentification with all such forms and delusions.

This destruction of delusion occurs as a result of the inquiry into the Self. Illusion is the product of ignorance. Ignorance is composed solely of false notions. The notions appear only so long as the Truth is not known. The ever-present Truth appears as if unknown only so long as one does not examine these false notions in the light of Knowledge. The light of Knowledge shines for one who inquires. Thus, by inquiry the Truth is known, false notions are discarded, ignorance vanishes, and illusion is realized to be nonexistent. Therefore, in *Who am I?*, Sri Bhagavan states, "If the ego arises, all else will also arise; if it subsides, all else will also subside."

If one inquires into the nature of the Self as the Maharshi has instructed, one is liberated from all ignorance, the three bodies, the five sheaths, the ego in any of its forms, and from all bondage. By such inquiry, one realizes the Self and abides as the one Absolute. By such inquiry, the Knowledge of the Guru abides in one's heart. By such inquiry, Reality is known.

May all inquire into the Self and, by the unending grace of Sri Bhagavan, abide in infinite Wisdom and Bliss. Whoever inquires as instructed by the Maharshi removes the false belief of being an individual entity in any kind of form or body and, being free of all coverings, shines in infinite Wisdom and Bliss.

Om Sri Ramanarpanamastu
Om May this be an offering to Sri Ramana

6

Disciple: While there are different modifications of the internal organ, viz., manas (reflection), buddhi (intellect), chitta (memory), and ahankara (egoity), how can it be said that the destruction of the mind alone is release?

The Maharshi: In the books explaining the nature of the mind, it is thus stated: "The mind is formed by the concretion of the subtle portion of the food we eat; it grows with the passions such as attachment and aversion, desire and anger; being the aggregate of the mind, intellect, memory, and egoity, it receives the collective, singular name 'mind'; the characteristics that it bears are thinking, determining, etc.; since it is an object of Consciousness (the Self), it is what is seen, inert; even though inert, it appears as if conscious because of association with Consciousness (like a red-hot iron ball); it is limited, non-eternal, partite, and changing like wax, gold, candle, etc.; it is of the nature of all elements (of phenomenal existence); its locus is the heart-lotus, even as the loci of the sense of sight, etc., are the eyes, etc.; it is the adjunct of the individual soul; thinking of an object, it transforms itself into a mode, and along with the knowledge that is in the brain, it flows through the five sense-channels, gets joined to objects by the brain (that is associated with knowledge), and thus knows and experiences objects and gains satisfaction. That substance is the mind."

Even as one and the same person is called by different names according to the different functions he performs, so also one and the same mind is called by the different names: mind, intellect, memory, and egoity, on account of the difference in the modes— and not because of any real difference. The mind itself is of the form of all, i.e., of soul, God, and world; when it becomes of the form of the Self through Knowledge, there is release, which is of the nature of Brahman: This is the teaching.

Commentary:
Om Namo Bhagavate Sri Ramanaya
The wise proclaim that the destruction of the mind alone is release. Destruction consists of the knowledge of its unreality, while release is Liberation from illusion. Illusion is a fabrication of the mind within the mind itself. The mind itself is an illusion. Illusions are destroyed by recognizing their unreality and by the direct experience, or Knowledge, of that which is real, as in the analogy of the rope and the snake in which the imagination of a snake, which is nonexistent, is superimposed on that which is actually present, the rope, and is destroyed by clear Knowledge.

The disciple who posed these questions raised them from a position of interest in teachings that he had read in various books, not all of the portions of which are advaita (nondual) in nature, and none of which are compositions by the Maharshi. In his answer, Sri Bhagavan compassionately gave explanations of what the texts state so that the disciple could comprehend what was written in those books, as well as expounded the Truth of the Self and the direct method of realizing the Self. Consequently, the first portion of the Maharshi's answer is simply a quotation of what the text says. The second portion is the Maharshi's actual answer. The Maharshi's answer is that which is essential; the other part contains the same points and also contains auxiliary explanations to suit the minds of those who may not, at first, grasp the significance of the teaching that one mind is all and that the nature of the mind is only the Self, or Brahman.

The text states the traditional observation of the yogis that what is consumed as food becomes part of the body, metabolized into subtler and subtler substances, and eventually, becoming entirely subtle, feeds or produces the mind. This may also be understood to apply to all that is experienced; all experiences are the food of the mind, or the subtle impressions of them, in the form of various thoughts, constitute the mind. The mind, which has no independent existence, seems to expand, or grow, in size by the conjuring up of its own delusions, which manifest in an extroverted mind as attachments. These appear in a dual manner, such as clinging and aversion, desire and anger, etc. All of these involve the superimposition of what is unreal and objective upon the Bliss of the Self. In other words, the innate happiness is projected by the mind upon its own thought forms, which may then be further delusively conceived as objects, which are but creations within the mind itself. The same ignorance appears as both sides of such duality.

The mind comprises all of the possible kinds of thoughts, patterns of thought, modes, and states of mind. No matter how it is analyzed and divided, it and all its parts are merely thought. Its many parts, aspects, and names are only more thoughts about itself. Thought, itself, is inert and has no knowing ability. Thought does not know itself. One thought does not know another thought. Thought is objective, the known. The knower, who can never be an object of knowledge, is Consciousness. Consciousness is the Self. The Self is not the mind. The mind appears as if a knowing entity in ignorance due to the misidentification of Consciousness, the eternal, nondual infinite Self, with thought. Like any objective thing, the mind appears as if with a form, is transient, is limited, and is divisible. Mutability is its nature. Immutability is the nature of the Self.

As a candle is but a temporary shape of wax and has no actual existence apart from the wax, as an ornament of gold is but a temporary shape of gold and has no actual existence apart from the gold, so the mind is but a form imagined in Consciousness that has no separate existence apart from Consciousness. However, unlike the phenomenal substances of gold and wax, Consciousness never undergoes any modification whatsoever. The notion that there is manifested Consciousness and unmanifested Consciousness remains only so long as one does not inquire into the knower of these. If the inquiry "Who am I?" is earnestly made, the individual "I," or "mind," vanishes, and, with it, all duality disappears, leaving the Self as the single, invariable Reality. Because it is associated with Consciousness, the mind appears to be aware, just as a red-hot iron ball appears to glow though there is no inherent heat or luminosity in the iron.

The mind comprises all of the elements and factors of experience. The entire phenomenal manifestation is in and of the mind. The mind itself ceases to be regarded as a mind once it is divested of all that is objective. What is objective is but a notion. A mind without notions is no mind at all.

Each of the senses is associated with a bodily location. Sight is associated with the eyes, hearing with the ears, and so forth and so on. The mind is associated with the brain. Upon deeper inquiry, though, the senses, along with their loci are comprehended as arising from the mind and occurring within the mind itself. Similarly, the mind, with its locus, appears within pure Consciousness alone. That Consciousness, of the nature of flawless perfection, is truly the Heart.

When the mind conceives of an object, that object appears. In the mind's illusion, conception of the object appears as if external to the mind, because, in delusion, the mind and one's identity are falsely assumed to be located within the body. The mind itself manifests as the five senses, with their corresponding organs and kinds of objects. Its conceiving is its supposed experiencing. The world is but the concept of it. By "satisfaction" is meant the process of the mind's creation of the desire for an objective experience and then, by its own conjuring, the fulfillment of that desire. The infinitesimal spark of happiness thereby experienced within the mind is but the faint reflection of the infinite Bliss of the Self. All of this process is merely sankalpa. All these sankalpa-s, as a whole, are termed the mind. The mind alone creates, experiences its own creations, and destroys them. The mind alone imagines itself to be.

The Maharshi, as the sadguru, bestowing the quintessence of Knowledge and always revealing the unobscured, direct way to realize the Self, then declares the teaching in his own gracious words. Blessed are the disciples who receive the teaching from the guru. Illumined by his Knowledge and immersed in his grace, their minds and sankalpa-s are destroyed without a trace remaining. By such a guru as Sri Bhagavan, one is doubtlessly liberated from the mind and ego and abides as the nondual Absolute, Brahman.

Sri Bhagavan lucidly points out that one and the same mind is given so many appellations due to the emphasis placed upon its functions. The variety of functions represents no multiplicity of minds. A person may be referred to by many terms according to situations and activities. He may be referred to by the kind of work or task in which he may be active, by the position among family members (father, son, brother, husband, uncle, grandfather, nephew, etc., or mother, sister, daughter, wife, aunt, grandmother, niece, etc.), by title of position, by affectionate names by friends, etc. The names vary according to the function. Similarly, the mind is given a variety of names that merely label its functions.

The Maharshi declares that the mind, itself, is of the form of all. It is the substance of all. All is its form. The individual, (jiva or soul), the world (inclusive of all matter, energy, occurrences, time, and space), and God are all forms of the mind. The mind, itself, appears as these. If the mind becomes of the form of the Self, these three—the individual, world, and God—indeed, all, cease as such, and the all-pervading Self, of the nature of Being-Consciousness-Bliss, is realized to be the ever-present Reality. The Self, though, has no form whatsoever. It is formless. Therefore, to "become the form of the Self" signifies the realization of the nature of the mind to be the Self alone. That is the realization that Consciousness alone is. In ignorance, it is imagined to be a mind. In Knowledge, Consciousness is known and experienced as it truly is: formless, nondual, eternal, and infinite. The Self alone is real, and the Self alone exists. There is nothing other than the Self, ever. Therefore, this Knowledge is Self-Knowledge, wherein the Consciousness that knows is itself the known. It knows itself; there is no other to do so.

The same essential, spiritual instruction appears in *Who am I?,* in which the Maharshi states, "By a steady and continuous investigation into the nature of the mind, the mind is transformed into That to which the "I" refers; and that is verily the Self. The mind has necessarily to depend for its existence upon something gross; it never subsists by itself. It is this mind that is otherwise called the subtle body, the ego, the jiva, or the soul." In reference to how this "I," by whatever name called, causes the one Reality to appear as if divided into the triad mentioned in this section and that the abidance in the state which is void of this "I" is best of all, the Maharshi later said in *Saddarshanam* (translation by Sri A. R. Natarajan), "All religions begin with the existence of the individual, the world, and God. So long as the ego lasts, these three will remain separate; to abide egoless, in the Self, is the best."

This Realization is of the nature of Knowledge. Knowledge does not create; it reveals. What it reveals is Reality. Reality is formless and uncreated. Reality is one without a second. It is not in relation to anything else whatsoever. "Anything else," such as a "mind," "phenomena," etc., is unreal. The unreal never comes to be. The Reality ever is. It is absolute. That is Brahman. That is the Self. This Realization

32

is Release, or Liberation, from all of the imagined bondage. This is the Truth and the nondual teaching.

Whoever is thus liberated, having imbibed the immortal nectar of the guru's instruction, is one with Brahman and, being free from the mind, is perpetually absorbed in infinite Wisdom and Bliss.

Om Sri Ramanarpanamastu
Om May this be an offering to Sri Ramana

7

Disciple: If these four—mind, intellect, memory, and egoity—are one and the same, why are separate locations mentioned for them?

The Maharshi: It is true that the throat is stated to be the location of the mind, the face or the heart of the intellect, the navel of the memory, and the heart or sarvanga of the egoity; though differently stated thus, yet for the aggregate of these, that is, the mind or internal organ, the location is the heart alone. This is conclusively declared in the scriptures.

Commentary:

Om Namo Bhagavate Sri Ramanaya

Whatever be the path by which the disciple approaches, the guru points him in the direction of the Truth, revealing the illusory nature of differentiation and the reality of the nondual Consciousness. Whatever be the concept in the disciple's mind, the Maharshi unfailingly reveals the Truth beyond all concepts and notions, beyond all time and space.

Sri Bhagavan has already shown how all the names of the mind refer to different views, aspects, or functions of the mind itself. Once they are differentiated and treated as separate, they will be given various attributes, such as location. Yet, all this is conceived within the mind itself. According to certain schools of yoga, these functions, conceived as separate entities, have specific locations. The disciple was evidently familiar with these, perhaps from the books upon which he asked Sri Bhagavan to comment. The Maharshi reiterates what is stated therein. "Sarvanga" signifies pervading the whole body. When one is in delusion, the ego seems to inhabit the entirety of the body, misidentifying with it. Upon inquiry into the nature of the Self, one realizes that the Self is not the body. One also realizes that the ego is not the body and does not occupy a location in the body. It is neither in a specific part nor all throughout the body. The ego is not physical in nature. The ego actually has no location at all, and its nature is nonexistence. As for the Self, it also has no location, but is omnipresent and ever existent.

When, as the Maharshi has declared, all the functions of the mind are known to be simply the mind itself, one then further realizes that the mind is contained in the heart. What is the heart? It is That which transcends all form, notions of inner and outer, and all notions of any other kind. It is Absolute Being, Brahman. This is explained in the Maharshi's next answer.

Whoever is blessed with grace of receiving the teachings of Sri Bhagavan, no matter what state it is in which he initially receives it, and practices those teachings ardently, no matter what state it is from which he is being liberated, finds the true nature of the Self and, being thus illumined, realizes his identity as that Self and thus abides in infinite Wisdom and Bliss.

Om Sri Ramanarpanamastu
Om May this be an offering to Sri Ramana

8

Disciple: Why is it said that only the mind, which is the internal organ, shines as of the form of all, that is, of soul, God, and world?

The Maharshi: As instruments for knowing the objects, the sense organs are outside, and so they are called outer senses; and the mind is called the inner sense because it is inside. But the distinction between inner and outer is only with reference to the body; in truth, there is neither inner nor outer. The mind's nature is to remain pure like ether. What is referred to as the heart or the mind is a collocation of the elements (of phenomenal existence) that appear as inner and outer. So, there is no doubt that all phenomena consisting of names and forms are of the nature of mind alone. All that appear outside are, in reality, inside and not outside; it is in order to teach this that in the Veda-s, also, all have been described as of the nature of the heart. What is called the heart is none other than Brahman.

Commentary:

Om Namo Bhagavate Sri Ramanaya

It is only in reference to the body that the world of sense objects is regarded as external and the mind with its objects of conception regarded as internal. When one ceases to misidentify with the body, the notions of inner and outer vanish.

The phenomenal world is experienced solely as the knowledge of it. The knowledge of it is solely of the nature of sense perception. It is by such sense perception that one has any experience or knowledge of an object, inclusive of the objects of the body and the sense organs themselves. The sense perceptions are known by and in the mind and nowhere else. Therefore, one and the same mind manifests as the senses and the objects and conceives of such differences.

In reference to the body, the mind is considered inner because of its subtler nature. The mind, itself, though, conceives of the body, the outside and the inside, and the gross and the subtle. None of these have any existence apart from the mind.

As in a dream, all the names and forms, the "outer perceptions" and "inner thoughts," the gross and the subtle, etc., are entirely contained within the dreaming mind, have no existence apart from the dreaming mind, and are composed solely of the dreaming state of mind, so is it with all that appears in the waking state in relation to the waking state of mind. It may be said that all of these elements and factors of experience (tattva-s) together compose the experience of that state, or it may be said the state is itself that which composes all of these. The meaning is the same: all is in the mind alone. The wise know all names and forms, all thoughts and perceptions, to be only the mind itself. So, in a passage contained within *Who am I?*, the Maharshi reiterates this wisdom, saying, "Nor is there any such thing as the physical world apart from and independent of thought. In deep sleep there are no thoughts; nor is there the world. In the wakeful and dream states, thoughts are present, and there is also the world. Just as a spider draws out the thread of the cobweb from within itself and withdraws it again into itself, even so out of itself the mind projects the world and absorbs it back into itself. The world is perceived as an apparent objective reality when the mind is externalized, thereby forsaking its identity with the Self. When the world is thus perceived, the true nature of the Self is not revealed; conversely, when the Self is realized, the world ceases to appear as an objective reality."

The Maharshi proclaims the truth that there is, in reality, no inner or outer. He declares the nature of the mind to be pure like space. Pure means unalloyed, while like space means it is inherently boundaryless and untouched by form. As space pervades all but remains unconfined by all, so the mind pervades all but is unconfined by that which is conjured up within itself. The mind remains pure, which means it is unalloyed—unmixed with anything else. If the mind does not mix with any object, then, negating the notions of objectivity as being delusions, what remains of the mind?

The dissolution of the mind is by Knowledge of the Self. Self-inquiry reveals it. The dissolution of that primary illusion, of a supposedly existent mind, is also the dissolution of subsidiary illusions within and based on it, such as the objective sphere of experience termed "the world." Thus, in *Who am I?*, the Maharshi reveals this wisdom in a manner similar to this section of *Self-Inquiry*, "If the mind, which is the instrument of knowledge and is the basis of all activity, subsides, the perception of the world as an objective reality ceases. Unless the illusory perception of the serpent in the rope ceases, the rope on which the illusion is formed is not perceived as such. Even so, unless the illusory nature of the perception of the world as an objective reality ceases, the vision of the true nature of the Self, on which the illusion is formed, is not obtained."

The nature of the mind is known by the wise. The knowledge of the nature of all is known by the wise. This entire universe and the entirety of the mind are completely of the nature of pure Consciousness. Consciousness is our quintessential Being. That is the Self. It is called the Heart. The Heart, the Self, is all in all at all times. It is One without a second. There is no duality at any time. The one Self, or Heart, alone is, eternally.

The one Self alone is imagined to be divided into jagat-jiva-para, the world, the individual, and the Supreme. The one Self alone is imagined to be a jivatman (individual self) and a Paramatman (Supreme Self). In Self-Knowledge, differentiation is realized to be unreal, and the forever-unmodified, nondual Being is realized to be what is real.

That Self is Brahman. Brahman is ineffable, formless, nondual, inconceivable Absolute Being. It is, and it alone is. From the Vedic rishi-s to the Maharshi, the Truth of the Self—of Brahman—has been revealed to be the nondual Reality.

Whoever receives and understands, by his Grace, this perfect Knowledge revealed by Sri Bhagavan, transcends the senses and their objects, dissolves the notions of inner and outer, and, becoming ethereal like space, realizes the Self, the Heart, and thus abides in infinite Wisdom and Bliss.

Om Sri Ramanarpanamastu
Om May this be an offering to Sri Ramana

9

Disciple: How can it be said that the heart is none other than Brahman?

The Maharshi: Although the Self enjoys its experiences in the states of waking, dream, and deep sleep, residing respectively in the eyes, throat, and heart, in reality, however, it never leaves its principal seat, the heart. In the heart-lotus, which is of the nature of all, in other words in the mind-ether, the light of that Self in the form "I" shines. As it shines thus in everybody, this very Self is referred to as the witness (sakshi) and the transcendent (turiya, literally the fourth). The "I"-less supreme Brahman, which shines in all bodies as interior to the light in the form of "I" is the Self-ether (or Knowledge-ether): That alone is the Absolute Reality. This is the super-transcendent (turiyatita). Therefore, it is stated that what is called the heart is none other than Brahman. Moreover, for the reason that Brahman shines in the hearts of all souls as the Self, the name "Heart" is given to Brahman. The meaning of the word "hridayam" when split thus "hrit-ayam" is, in fact, Brahman. The adequate evidence for the fact that Brahman, which shines as the Self, resides in the hearts of all is that all people indicate themselves by pointing to the chest when saying "I."

Commentary:

Om Namo Bhagavate Sri Ramanaya

Sri Bhagavan abides in Brahman as Brahman. His word is Brahman's declaration about itself. His Silence is the vast, eternal Silence of Brahman. Brahman, in the form of the wondrous Guru, Sri Ramana Maharshi, has revealed the truth about Brahman. He who dwells in the hearts of all has proclaimed the true nature of the heart itself: the heart is Brahman. That is, Brahman is one's quintessential Being.

The Guru is compassion and Grace incarnate and untiringly reveals the nondual Truth to the disciple who, earnest and humble, is desirous of the Realization of the Self, Brahman, in order to attain Liberation from all of the imagined bondage. In the course of instruction, the Guru thoroughly explains the Truth, and, while presenting it in such a way as the disciple is capable of understanding, never swerves from his ever-consistent Realization of the nondual Truth. Innumerable lifetimes of hopes and prayers for happiness and peace, of striving to wake up from this illusion, of attempting to meditate upon the Truth, are answered by finding Sri Bhagavan, to be immersed in Wisdom and Bliss.

Within infinite Consciousness, which is the Self, three states of mind appear, each one temporarily eliminating the previous one successively. These are the states of waking, dream, and deep sleep. The illusion of subject and object and of the triads (experiencer, experiencing, and the object experienced) appear in the waking and dream states. In deep sleep, these are completely absent. An individual "I," to whom these states occur, manifests in the waking and dream states and remains unmanifest in the deep sleep state. If the nature of this "I" is inquired into, it loses its individuality, and the Self alone remains. Without such inquiry, there is no Self-Knowledge. Without Self-Knowledge, the "I" appears as if an individual entity—it appears to leave its true abode of the Heart, which is Brahman—and becomes further misidentified with a form. That form is usually a body, a body that corresponds to the state of mind then present. In Reality, though, the Self is ever as it is. It never becomes an ego-entity, nor does it become embodied. It is ever stateless, and, in it, no mind has ever come to be. It abides forever in the Heart. That is, Being is ever unmoving and never differentiated from itself.

In compassion for the disciple familiar with certain lore, Sri Bhagavan refers to the eyes, etc., as the places assigned to the experiencer's subtle position according to the state of mind. These positions, however, are stated in texts from the perspective of the waking state only. Moreover, when the nature of the experiencer is known and one is thus liberated from misidentification with the body and the mind, the unmoving, all-pervading, locationless nature of the true Self is realized.

The Heart is the nature of all. Lotus signifies its spiritual perfection. That which is the nature of all is transcendent of form. In the infinite space of pure Consciousness, the illusion of the mind-space appears. It appears as a causal state of deep sleep, within which arises the capacity to dream. Within the apparently unending maya of these dreams, one dream is designated as the waking state. The Self shines as the sense of "I" within all of this mind-space. The Light of the Self is pure Consciousness. Holding onto the "I" and tracing it to its very existence as unmodified Consciousness is the essence of the inquiry. This Consciousness is the very Being of all. Considered in relation to all beings, it is the very identity of all. This Self is always present and not at all divided from oneself.

This Self is the silent, perpetually present witness of all. It can never be an object of perception or conception. It transcends all the states of mind and their contents. Thus, it is called "the Fourth" (turiya). Consciousness in relation to all else is known as the witness. When all is known to be unreal, even its witness-hood no longer applies, and it remains as the egoless supreme Brahman. That is the infinite space of the Self. Its nature is pure Knowledge. In Self-Knowledge, Being is itself the Knowledge. This Knowledge-space is devoid of the triad of knower-knowing-known. This Self is alone the Reality, one without a second. It transcends even every idea of transcendence and is never conditioned or modified in any manner whatsoever. So, it is called turiyatita (beyond the fourth).

Therefore, the Self itself shines as "I" within all. It is the ever-present witness of all. Though it appears as if in three states, the three states actually appear in it. If this "I" is inquired into and one realizes its innermost nature, it is the vast, formless Absolute. That is Brahman. That is the Self. That alone exists and is real. To realize the Self in the Heart means to abide as That. Abidance is Self-Knowledge. So, the Maharshi declares that what is called the heart is none other than Brahman.

Brahman is the Self of all. There is no other kind of self. In *Talks with Sri Ramana Maharshi,* entry 97 dated November 19, 1935, the Maharshi says, "Hridayam means Hritayam [which] means This is the Center," and, "Brahman is the Heart." In *Talks with Sri Ramana Maharshi,* entry 474 dated March 16, 1938, Sri Bhagavan explains, "The Heart of the Upanishads is construed as Hridayam meaning: this (is) the center. That is, it is where the mind rises and subsides." The significance is that Brahman is the Self. "Heart" is the name given to that ineffable, nondual Reality. These instructions by the Maharshi may be in reference to *Chandogya Upanishad* 8:3:3, "He, indeed, this Self, surely exists in the heart. Of that, this is, indeed, the explicit interpretation. It is in the heart; therefore, that is called the heart." In *Talks with Sri Ramana Maharshi,* entry 252 dated September 30, 1936, he says, "To remain as one's Self is to enter the Heart." Thus abidance as the Self, which is Self-Knowledge, is abidance in Brahman. Similarly, in *Talks with Sri Ramana Maharshi,* entry 403 dated April 17, 1937, he says, "You are, and it is a fact. Dhyana (meditation) is by you, of you, and in you. It must go on where you are. It cannot be outside you. So, you are the center of dhyana, and that is the Heart;" and "Heart is only another name for the Self." Therefore, if the meditation be upon the nature of the meditator, that is, Self-inquiry, the Self, which is Brahman, is realized.

When a person says "I" and attempts to indicate himself, he or she usually points to the chest area of the body. However, if that person is asked, "Do you mean to say that this surface skin is yourself?" he will say, "No." "Then the flesh beneath?" "No." "The bones?" "No." "The blood, etc.?" "No." "The cells?" "No." "Just this physical spot?" "No." The physical gesture simply indicates something interior, but not something physical. How is one to physically point out something nonphysical in nature?

What, then, is indicated? It is something immediately present and within. To what does "I" refer? The "I" is not the body, not the senses, not the prana, and not mind and intellect. It is not anything of the three states. Sri Bhagavan has revealed the Truth of the Self: it is formless, timeless, birthless, deathless, unmodified, immutable Being-Consciousness-Bliss. Whether it is called "the Self," "the Heart," or "Brahman," it is the sole-existent Reality.

Dive within to realize the Self. As the witness, remain unattached to all, and transcendent of all thought, know the Self as it is. Those who do so, by His Grace and all-comprehensive Knowledge, abide in infinite Wisdom and Bliss.

Om Sri Ramanarpanamastu
Om May this be an offering to Sri Ramana

10

Disciple: If the entire universe is of the form of the mind, then does it not follow that the universe is an illusion?

If that be the case, why is the creation of the universe mentioned in the Veda?

The Maharshi: There is no doubt whatsoever that the universe is the merest illusion. The principal purport of the Veda is to make known the true Brahman after showing the apparent universe to be false. It is for this purpose that the Veda-s admit the creation of the world and not for any other reason. Moreover, for the less qualified persons, creation is taught, that is the staged evolution of prakriti, mahatattva, tanmatra-s, bhuta-s, the world, the body, etc., from Brahman; while for the more qualified, simultaneous creation is taught, that is, that this world arose like a dream on account of one's own thoughts induced by the defect of not knowing oneself as the Self. Thus, from the fact that the creation of the world has been described in different ways, it is clear that the purport of the Veda-s rests only in teaching the true nature of Brahman after showing somehow or other the illusory nature of the universe. That the world is illusory, every one can directly know in the state of Realization, which is in the form of experience of one's bliss-nature.

Commentary:
Om Namo Bhagavate Sri Ramanaya

Sri Bhagavan abides as That, Brahman, wholly transcendent of all form. His state is his Being, and this Being is free of creation, forever unmanifested, of the nature of unalloyed, nondual Consciousness-Bliss. Ever abiding as That, he appears as the guru, the guru who is beyond the world and graciously awakens one from the dream-like illusion of the world, and who is beyond the mind and compassionately awakens one from the illusion of the mind.

The Maharshi has already revealed that all phenomena appear only in the mind and are of the nature of the mind itself. The disciple, pursuing the guru's precious instructions, perceives that the world, being but the product of the mind's conjuring and having no separate or external reality, must necessarily be an illusion. The question then arises: if the universe is an illusion, why have the Veda-s and other scriptures, the purpose of which is to reveal the Truth, given elaborate details concerning the manner of creation?

The Maharshi commences his all-illuminating answer by declaring the unreal nature of the universe and by proclaiming that the purpose of the Veda is the elucidation of the Knowledge of Brahman, the nondual Absolute. What is referred to as "the universe," or "the world," includes all forms, subtle and gross. It includes all objects, all sentient beings, all events, all matter and energy, and all that is perceptible and conceivable. All of that, without exception, is declared to be unreal—utterly illusory and nonexistent—by the knowers of Truth.

Brahman alone is. It is the one undifferentiated Existence that ever is as it is, free of all modification. It has neither within nor without, beginning nor end, creation nor destruction. Described as Being-Consciousness-Bliss, it transcends all objectivity, all thought, and all differentiated experience. They who realize it are it, for there is no such duality as knower and known.

It is this one Existence that, in delusion, is conceived as a differentiated world, as a rope is imagined to be a snake in a dimly lit room. The illusion of a world depends upon the illusion of a separate seer. If the true nature of the seer is known, individuality, being false, vanishes, and with it disappears the world illusion. So, in *Who am I?*, the Maharshi again states, "When the world is thus perceived, the true nature of the Self is not revealed; conversely, when the Self is realized, the world ceases to appear as an objective reality."

Therefore, in *Vivekacudamani*, Adi Sankara states, verse 292,

यत्रैष जगदाभासः दर्पणान्तः पुरं यथा ।
तद् ब्रह्माहमिति ज्ञात्वा कृतकृत्यो भविष्यसि । ।

yatraiṣa jagadābhāsaḥ darpaṇāntaḥ puraṁ yathā |
tad brahmāhamiti jñātvā kṛtakṛtyo bhaviṣyasi ||

which may be translated as, "Where this reflection of the world is as a city within a mirror, having known thus, 'I

43

am Brahman,' you will be (one who is) fully accomplished (fully realized, with full attainment)." Similarly, in verse 294,

सर्वात्मना दृश्यमिदं मृषैव नैवाहमर्थः क्षणिकत्वदर्शनात् ।
जानाम्यहं सर्वमिति प्रतीतिः कुतोऽहमादेः क्षणिकस्य सिद्ध्येत् ॥

sarvātmanā dṛśyamidaṁ mṛṣaiva naivāhamarthaḥ
    kṣaṇikatvadarśanāt |
jānāmyahaṁ sarvamiti pratītiḥ kuto'hamādeḥ kṣaṇikasya
    siddhyet ||

which may be translated as, "With the Self, which is all, this, the seen (this perceived) is false. Not, indeed, is 'I' the truth (real), for its momentariness is seen. 'I know all,' thus: how can [this] ascertainment be valid of the momentary 'I,' etc.?"

If one misidentifies with the illusion, Brahman is not seen. If one is liberated from such misidentification, one realizes that Brahman alone is, and there is neither illusion nor a seer of it.

The Realization of Brahman is vast peace and bliss. It is immortality and complete freedom. It is abidance in our natural state.

The purpose of the scriptures is an exalted and glorious one. They appear for the revelation of the eternal, not merely the transient, the revelation of the Absolute, not mere relative conception. They cannot be intended for a description of duality, for such dualism is already the view of the spiritual aspirant and reiteration of the same would merely foster maya and samsara. Rather, nondual Truth must be the basis, purpose, and teaching of the scriptures, for the Realization of such is blissful immortality. The Vedas and similar sacred texts have as their purpose the revelation of Brahman. The endless teachings and passages contained in them have for their ultimate purpose the revelation of Brahman. Some passages are immediate revelations, some gradual, but the ultimate purpose remains the same. Therefore, descriptions of creation are intended to guide one to creation's source. The source can never be defined in terms of its effect. Brahman is ineffable and indefinable by worldly or objective notions.

Sri Bhagavan states two general approaches taken by the scriptures relating to creation. The first assumes, for the sake of the aspirant who as of yet does not comprehend a higher view, that the world has actually come to be. How has it come to be? The descriptions are various, but involve prakrti ("primal nature," manifestation; or the substance of which all forms are made), mahat-tattva (an initial great principle or intelligence that brings forth creation—the Maharshi has stated that it is the projected light from Absolute Consciousness); the tanmatra-s, which are the five subtle elements corresponding to the five forms of sense experience (smell with subtle earth, taste with subtle water, form with subtle fire, touch with subtle air, and sound with subtle space); the bhuta-s (five gross elements: earth, water, fire, air, space); and the combination of all of the above to form a world and a body appearing in such a world. From there, the individual bodily experiences extend. All of that, in all its complexity and permutations, for however long appearing, is from Brahman and Brahman alone. The effect is nothing other than its cause; the cause itself appears as the effect. Brahman, being the one cause of all, alone constitutes this entire universe.

The second approach presented by Sri Bhagavan, simultaneous creation, is comprehensible by those who are more steeped in wisdom. In this, the world is declared to be like a dream, produced by one's own thoughts. If the Self is known, one is free from thoughts. In the Reality of the Self, even the first thought has not yet arisen and no differentiation, dream-like or otherwise, has ever come to be. If the Self is not known, Consciousness, which is the Self, appears as if differentiated into countless thoughts and a knower of them, who remains unseen. When the knower, who is nonobjective, is known, he is pure Consciousness unalloyed with any thought or form.

Thought alone constitutes the experience of all form. There is no sense perception apart from the mind that knows those perceptions. There are no forms apart from those perceptions. There is no world apart from those forms. The body is thought. The gross and subtle are thought. Time and space are only thought. Inside and outside are only thought. All things perceived at all times are only thought. Thus, in a similar passage of *Who am I?*, Sri Bhagavan says, "The phenomenal world is nothing but thought. When the world recedes from one's view, that is when free from thought, the mind enjoys the Bliss of the Self. Conversely, when the world appears, that is when thought occurs, the mind experiences pain and anguish." Likewise, in *Saddarshanam*, verse six concludes (translation by Sri A. R. Natarajan), "Therefore, the world is but the mind."

A dream is composed of thought. Its supposed "reality" is due solely to the projection of this "reality" from Consciousness, which is true Being, upon thoughts. In a dream, neither the dream character nor the dream world is real. The only real substance, composing the entire dream, is Consciousness; this Consciousness is the one thing that never appears as a dream form. That is, Consciousness, which alone constitutes the dream, is the one thing never seen in the dream. But when one awakens, one knows, "All that was a dream: it was all only my mind," and the Consciousness, which was present in the previous state, remains, unchanged, in the waking state. Similarly, Consciousness, which is the Self, composes the entire waking state experience, inclusive of the entire universe, but never appears as any particular form in this universe. When one awakens in Self-Knowledge, this dream-like world is known as entirely illusory, and one realizes that pure Being-Consciousness-Bliss alone exists.

Regarding the dream-like nature of the waking state experience, which is erroneously conceived as a world, the Maharshi states, in *Who am I?*, "He should, on the other hand, consider the phenomenal world with reference to himself as merely a dream. Except that the wakeful state is long and the dream state is short, there is no other difference between them. All the activities of the dream state appear, for the time being, just as real as the activities of the wakeful state seem to be while awake. Only, during the dream state, the mind assumes another form or a different bodily sheath. For, thoughts on the one hand, and name and form on the other, occur simultaneously during the wakeful and dream states."

What is illusion does not exist in any manner whatsoever at any time. That which is Reality never ceases to be and never becomes other than what it is.

The all-knowing, ever gracious Sri Ramana, the one who liberates and is the dweller in the Heart, then describes the purport of the Vedas again. The fact that creation is described by the authoritative scriptures in a variety of ways is itself proof of the employment of a multitude of perspectives and that none are the final Truth. The ultimate intention of all of them is to teach the true nature of Brahman—the infinite, eternal, Absolute Being. Many are the ways of revealing the illusory nature of the world. The direct experience of Brahman is singular.

The actual understanding of the nature of the world comes only by direct experience. Since, as has already been shown, the world has no independent existence, direct experience consists of experience of the Self, of the nature of Being-Consciousness. Such experience, being beyond the senses and thought, is of the nature of pure Knowledge. That Knowledge invariably reveals the nondual Truth for all beings. Such Realization is profound, unending happiness and peace. Wherever Being is, there is Consciousness. Wherever Being is, there is Bliss. Being-Consciousness-Bliss are three terms used to indicate the indivisible, ineffable Reality of the Self. Whoever realizes Being dwells in immortal Bliss.

The Maharshi has declared, at a later time, that all of the sastra-s (scriptures) are based upon the ego, the destruction of which is their purpose. Thus, if the ego is taken to exist as an embodied form, the grand creation of the universe is taught to reveal the illimitable immensity of the Supreme, and the ego is thus attenuated and drawn to the Source. If the ego is taken to exist, yet misidentification with the body is not prevailing, all this is shown as a mere dream, and the ego is thus dissolved as the objectifying outlook is abandoned, and one transcends the states of mind that could give rise to such illusion. If the ego is not existent at all, in the Realization of the Unborn, no-creation is the self-evident fact, and the scriptural explanations of the final Truth relate to this. Therefore, in verse four of *Saddarshanam* (translation by Sri A. R. Natarajan), the Maharshi proclaims, "When one is the formless Self, who is there to see?"

In Gambhiram Seshayya's original notebook, as mentioned by B.V. Narasimha Swami, the Maharshi concludes this section with: "It is by the Self being clouded by avarana (veiling of ignorance) that this dreamlike, illusory, or phenomenal world appears. In reality, though, the Self is not covered. It only appears to be covered to the eye of persons who are under the impression that they are the body."

Thus, when the world is conceived, the Self is not known. When the Self is known as it is, the world is not imagined. One Existence alone is. With the veil of ignorance, it appears as if a multiplicity. Free of ignorance, the formless Existence is as it is. The veil of ignorance, also, is not real, as the one Self alone exists eternally. This is the original intention of the holy scriptures. This is what Sri Bhagavan has revealed. He, whose nature is ineffable, has thus graciously revealed the ineffable Truth. He who transcends the world has thus shown its nature. Revealing the Self, he has revealed himself. Yet no one can know that, for if one knows that, individuality is forever lost, and nothing remains but Him, the Self.

Whoever, with a heart full of devotion and endowed with an intense desire for Self-Realization, absorbs so much as a drop of the nectar of the Maharshi's supreme, sublime teaching, realizes the uncreated, worldless Truth, and thus abides, no doubt, in infinite Wisdom and Bliss.

Om Sri Ramanarpanamastu
Om May this be an offering to Sri Ramana

11

Disciple: Is Self-experience possible for the mind, whose nature is constant change?

The Maharshi: Since sattva guna (the constituent of prakriti that makes for purity, intelligence, etc.) is the nature of the mind and since the mind is pure and undefiled like ether, what is called "mind" is, in truth, of the nature of knowledge. When it stays in that natural (i.e., pure) state, it has not even the name "mind." It is only the erroneous knowledge that mistakes one for another that is called mind. What was (originally) the pure sattva mind, of the nature of pure knowledge, forgets its knowledge-nature on account of nescience, gets transformed into the world under the influence of tamo-guna (i.e., the constituent of prakriti that makes for dullness, inertness, etc.), being under the influence of rajo-guna (i.e., the constituent of prakriti that makes for activity, passions, etc.), imagines "I am the body, etc.; the world is real," acquires the consequent merit and demerit through attachment, aversion, etc., and, through the residual impressions (vasana-s) thereof, attains birth and death. But the mind that has got rid of its defilement through action without attachment performed in many past lives, listens to the teaching of scripture from a true guru, reflects on its meaning, and meditates in order to gain the natural state of the mental mode of the form of the Self, i.e., of the form "I am Brahman," which is the result of the continued contemplation of Brahman.

Commentary:
Om Namo Bhagavate Sri Ramanaya

Prostrations to the true guru, the divine sage, who shines with the immortal Knowledge of the Self. He reveals the mind to be an empty illusion. He reveals pure, homogeneous Consciousness to be the one reality. He destroys inertia and agitation and then causes the sattvic mind, inclined toward the light of Knowledge, to dissolve into its real nature—that Absolute Consciousness. He destroys the confusion regarding the real and the unreal. He, who is the Self dwelling in the hearts of all, shows the unreal to be ever nonexistent and the Real to ever be.

Those who seek the truth turn their minds inward in order to realize the Self. The Realization, or Knowledge, of the Self is of the nature of direct, non-conceptual, nonobjective experience. The Self is formless, not to be perceived as a gross or subtle object, and utterly transcendent of all thought. The mind is involved in notions, is composed of thought—with each thought being of an objective character, gross or subtle—and is characterized by constant change. Therefore, the earnest disciple supplicates the guru for illumination as to how the changeful can experience the changeless, the form the formless, the notional the non-conceptual?

The Maharshi, with his inexhaustible grace and perfect Wisdom that know no bounds, begins to explain the answer to the great mystery.

All manifestation or prakriti is said to be of the three guna-s or qualities: tamas, inertia and dullness; rajas, active, agitated, and passionate; and sattva, pure, endowed with the light of Knowledge, characterized by wakeful peace. Of all the manifestations, the mind is the subtlest. It is declared to be of the nature of sattva.

When the mind is still, intense, and serene, it is in its true state. Its stillness is its uncreated nature, its intensity is the ever-shining reality of pure Consciousness, and its serenity is of immutable Being. If the nature of the mind is known, purely as it is, it is found to be like space, for it is without limit, of no form, all-pervading, containing all, colorless and shapeless, immeasurable, and indivisible. Such a mind is really pure Consciousness. Consciousness is, itself, Knowledge. There is nothing else that knows other than Consciousness. Consciousness is the only knower. It is Knowledge itself. In truth, it is the only known. In Self-Realization, the three are not three; one Consciousness alone is, and that is self-effulgent. There is no ignorance in it and no division into qualities. It is declared to be supreme Knowledge.

The natural state of mind is that which is free of all ignorance. Ignorance alone is the cause of imagined bondage, duality, and differentiation—inclusive of the dualistic, binding notion of a differentiated mind. In the Knowledge free from ignorance, there is no individual mind. The mind in its natural state is pure Consciousness. It has neither form nor name. How can we call That a "mind"?

What, then, is referred to by the term "mind"? It is simply the "erroneous knowledge that mistakes one for another." The confounding of the real and the unreal is the mind. The confounding of the ego and the Self is the mind. The confounding of thought for knowledge is the mind. The superimposition of objective characteristics upon the nonobjective Self is the mind. Misidentification is the mind.

The pure sattva mind, which is Consciousness alone, is able to realize "Self-experience." The Realization is the repose in its own nature. The mind's original state is That. That is immutable. The original is the ever present, but, in delusion, it appears otherwise. The very same mind, in nescience, forgets its own nature and is plagued by rajas and tamas. Rajas displays itself as agitation in the midst of space-like serenity, as thoughts, desires, etc., in the midst of the vast, space-like stillness of the Self. The mind in tamas, that is as inertia, itself appears as the world, inclusive of the form of the body, in the midst of the worldless, bodiless Self, while the imagination of rajas manifests the notion of the belief that one is the body and the world is real. As a result, the mind itself, engrossed in its own imaginings, mental and physical, is caught in the web of its own attachment, with its own veils of expectation and aversion, desire and fear. All this imagination, appearing as if solidified, is samsara, the repetitive cycle of birth and death. It is characterized by the illusion of suffering. Of what is it composed? It is composed of vasana-s, the tendencies that derive from such imagination and that perpetuate the same.

The Maharshi has summarized the instruction given here and contrasted ignorance and Knowledge in terms of extroversion and introversion of the mind in *Who am I?* thus, "It is only when the subtle mind is externalized through the activity of the intellect and the sense organs that gross name and form constituting the world appear. When, on the other hand, the mind stays and abides in the Heart, they (name and form) recede and disappear. Restraint of the out-going mind and its absorption in the Heart is known as introversion (antarmukha-drishti). The release of the mind and its emergence from the Heart is known as bahirmukha-drishti (objective-ness)."

Sri Bhagavan has thus, in brief, described the illusion. Illusion, being illusory and of no real substance, can be given any number of explanations. The explanations are as illusory as the illusion itself. Only such an explanation that serves to consume the illusion is wise. It will reveal the Truth, show the insubstantiality of a mirage, reveal the real nature of a rope-snake, and cause all dreams to vanish. Such is Sri Bhagavan's explanation given as compassionate help for the disciple. Now, he declares the means to destroy the ignorance and thus abide in true Knowledge.

Action without attachment alone creates no vasana-s. Rather, it yields the fruit of introversion for the mind. It yields humility and diminishes the ego. Action with attachment is productive only of more egoistic delusion. Attachment without action is delusion in the mind, without gross manifestation, but still binding. Nonattachment, with or without action, is liberating. He who acts without attachment can remain at one with the nondual Absolute at all times.

There are two ways to explain how a person can be so fortunate as to meet with a sadguru and be instructed in the Truth by him—the Truth that is exalted in the scriptures, the Realization of which is blissful immortality. It can be said that it occurs solely by grace. This in itself suffices as a complete explanation. Some, though, will ask, "How does one deserve such grace?" To them, the answer is given, "It is due to the selfless activity of the past, the nonattachment toward all else, that this grace has manifested." The true guru, who reveals the Truth, is grace manifest. In the case of one who cannot see what he has done so selflessly that he is so graced with a sadguru, the explanation is that such must have occurred at a previous time; therefore one must be certain to approach the guru and practice in such a manner that he does not waste now what may have required so long to attain.

The earnest disciple listens attentively to the teaching, forsaking all preconceptions and the mind's tendency to assume that its own notions are valid knowledge. The teaching finds an abode in the innermost recess of the disciple. By reflection upon the Truth, it is not forgotten or overshadowed by the notions of delusion. By meditation, one is absorbed in the Truth, and the mind that commences the meditation dissolves and vanishes in the process. Thus, the natural state of unalloyed Being-Consciousness-Bliss is realized. In the natural state, the mind is nothing but the Self.

The Self is Brahman, and one who knows the Self knows Brahman. The Self alone knows itself; Brahman alone knows itself. There is no other. The continuous contemplation or unbroken meditation on Brahman, in which the triad of meditator, meditating, and the object of meditation does not exist, reveals this natural state of the existence of the indivisible Self without a trace of anything else.

Whoever understands and practices the Maharshi's lucid instruction is liberated from all bondage of the mind. Whoever, with a heart full of devotion, and with nonattachment toward all else, listens to, reflects on, and deeply and continuously meditates on what the Maharshi has revealed finds his mind to be no mind whatsoever, but pure Consciousness alone, and, abiding in the only true state, realizes infinite Wisdom and Bliss.

Om Sri Ramanarpanamastu
Om May this be an offering to Sri Ramana

11

(continued)

The Maharshi: Thus will be removed the mind's transformation into the world in the aspect of tamoguna, and its roving therein in the aspect of rajo-guna. When this removal takes place, the mind becomes subtle and unmoving. It is only by the mind that is impure and is under the influence of rajas and tamas that Reality (i.e., the Self), which is very subtle and unchanging, cannot be experienced; just as a piece of fine silk cloth cannot be stitched with a heavy crowbar, or as the details of subtle objects cannot be distinguished by the light of a lamp flame that flickers in the wind. But in the pure mind that has been rendered subtle and unmoving by the meditation described above, the Self-bliss (i.e., Brahman) will become manifest. As without mind there cannot be experience, it is possible for the purified mind endowed with the extremely subtle mode (vritti) to experience the Self-bliss by remaining in that form (i.e., in the form of Brahman). Then, that one's Self is of the nature of Brahman will be clearly experienced.

Commentary:

Om Namo Bhagavate Sri Ramanaya

Obeisance to Sri Bhagavain, the guru who destroys all illusion, who absorbs the mind by revealing its true nature to be of infinite Consciousness, who reveals the nature of the Self in utmost clarity, and who is verily the one who awakens the disciple from the dream of maya, liberating the disciple from the bondage of delusion and saving him from the transmigratory suffering of samsara.

The Maharshi has previously revealed the path of listening to the guru, reflection, and profound meditation upon the Truth. This yields the Realization of the natural state. The natural state is the state of Self-Knowledge, or the Knowledge of Brahman. Brahman, or the Self, is nonobjective and nondual in nature. No one can remain apart from it to know it. In Self-Knowledge, knowing is Being. The natural state is that in which knowing the Self is being the Self. By being as you are—that is, abidance as unalloyed Being, free of any concept of individuality or duality—all the mind's delusion is removed, including the notion of an existent, differentiated mind.

The "differentiated mind" is a notion. An "individual experiencer" is a notion. An "embodied entity" is a notion. "The world" is a notion. Everything but the Self is a mere notion.

The true nature of the mind is pure Consciousness. When misidentification occurs in the form of conjuring up duality, which is but the superimposition of the notion of differentiation on the ever-indivisible Consciousness, it appears as if there is an existent mind separate from that infinite Consciousness. Within such a mind appears all the dream-like illusion. When the mind concocts illusions endowed with the guna (quality) of tamas (inertia), these illusions, which are but the mind itself, appear as the world. When the mind concocts illusions endowed with the guna of rajas (agitation), these illusions appear as the form of the sentient being, or mind, that roams through that world. Both these guna-s and their respective manifestations are only of the mind.

By intensely following the liberating instruction bestowed by the Maharshi, the mind's transformation into the world and the roving therein are destroyed, just as darkness is said to be removed or destroyed by the presence of light. The cessation of such transformation is the end of ignorance. Upon this cessation, the mind becomes subtle and unmoving. The mind appears to be a mind only so long as there is the grasping at the objects of thought and Consciousness is assumed to move or change with those mutable thoughts. If the mind is divorced from all objects of thought, what remains? The mind with nothing objective is pure Consciousness alone. If the mind is absorbed in that which is unmoving, what remains? Only the ever-still, pure Consciousness remains. Consciousness is subtle beyond all subtlety; it is utterly formless and is always motionless. It is never modified, and it never undergoes any kind of change.

The Self is naturally self-effulgent. Just as there is no cloud in the sun itself, so the Self, of the nature of ever-shining Consciousness, cannot be unknowing of itself. Who, then, suffers delusion and is ignorant of the Self? Only the mind that is "impure," that is caught in dualism and conceives its own transitory, unreal illusions to be real, is blind to the Self. The Self is nondual and completely formless. It cannot be apprehended by the form of a mind anymore than fine silk can be sewn with a crowbar. The Self is immutable. How can a mind that is like a flickering lamp—ever changing—apprehend it? If, though, the mind is pure, that is, bereft of dualistic notions, it is itself the formless and immutable, and being free from movement in the illusion of otherness, it is absorbed in the Self. The Self is pure Being-Consciousness-Bliss. The Self is Brahman. Or, we may consider the mind's flickering as the rajas quality and tamas as the blunt inertia quality, while it is a steady mind illumined by discrimination that is capable of pursuing the sadhana of inquiry and realizing the Truth.

The Bliss of the Self is without comparison. It is uncaused happiness. It is unfading joy. It is limitless. Realizing it, one desires nothing else. Absorption in it erases even the memory of suffering. For one who has realized the Self, absorbed in the Bliss thereof, grief and fear are impossible. Upon the Realization of the Self, this great Bliss is one's perpetual, direct experience.

This formless, unmoving, blissful state is revealed by meditation. To what meditation does Sri Bhagavan refer? To the meditation that establishes one in the natural state of Self-Realization. This is the inquiry into the Self—Who am I?—already elucidated by the Maharshi earlier in the text. This includes transcendence of the body and the "I"-notion, or ego. It also includes the preclusion of extroversion and the remaining as the transcendent witness, of the nature of unalloyed Consciousness. Alluding to this absorption of the mind by Self-inquiry and resultant Realization of true Silent Being, in *Who am I?* the Maharshi says, "If, in this manner, the mind becomes absorbed in the Heart, the ego or the 'I,' which is the center of the multitude of thoughts, finally vanishes, and pure Consciousness, or the Self, which subsists during all the states of the mind, alone remains resplendent. It is this state, in which there is not the slightest trace of the 'I' thought, that is the true Being of oneself. And that is called Quiescence or Mouna."

At the conclusion of His answer, the Maharshi dissolves the disciple's doubt from another perspective. If the belief of the disciple is that the mind is the knowing principle and that, therefore, without it there can be no experience whatsoever, to experience the Self, one should render the mind extremely subtle. If the mind reaches the furthest extent of subtlety, it will revel in the experience of Self-Bliss. But then, the only form of the mind is Brahman itself—space-like, vast Being, which is the Bliss, the Self, itself.

However the mind be approached, if it is introverted and its delusion is abandoned, one's own Self will be realized. The only purpose of any sadhana with the mind is to arrive at this Realization. It is the direct, clear experience of the Truth. The Truth is that the Self and Brahman, the Absolute, are one and the same without the least trace of differentiation whatsoever. That one Self, Brahman, alone exists eternally.

Whoever, with a heart full of devotion, keenly pursues the Maharshi's precious instruction, will dissolve the illusions of the mind, and being free of the guna-s and all the changeful, transitory, unreal forms, will abide, by His grace, in infinite Wisdom and Bliss.

Om Sri Ramanarpanamastu
Om May this be an offering to Sri Ramana

12

Commentary:

Om Namo Bhagavate Sri Ramanaya

May Sri Bhagavan, who is Siva himself, who reveals the true nature of the Self, graciously bless all who, by that grace, receive this sublime teaching of his, which is the non-dual Truth, with absorption in that Truth. One who remains thus absorbed, abides in the Self as the Self. Such is Self-Knowledge, which consists of direct, uninterrupted, perpetual experience of the Self, of the nature of unalloyed Being-Consciousness-Bliss.

Disciple: Is the aforesaid Self-experience possible, even in the state of empirical existence, for the mind, which has to perform functions in accordance with its prarabdha (the past karma that has begun to fructify)?

The Maharshi: A brahmin may play various parts in a drama, yet the thought that he is a brahmin does not leave his mind. Similarly, when one is engaged in various empirical acts, there should be the firm conviction "I am the Self" without allowing the false idea "I am the body, etc." to rise. If the mind should stray from its state, then immediately one should inquire, "Oh! Oh! We are not the body, etc! Who are we?" and thus one should reinstate the mind in that (pure) state. The inquiry "Who am I?" is the principal means to the removal of all misery and the attainment of the supreme bliss. When, in this manner, the mind becomes quiescent in its own state, Self-experience arises of its own accord without any hindrance. Thereafter, sensory pleasures and pains will not affect the mind. All (phenomena) will appear, then, without attachment, like a dream. Never forgetting one's plenary Self-experience is real bhakti (devotion), yoga (mind control), jnana (Knowledge), and all other tapas. Thus say the sages.

Commentary:

The Maharshi has already revealed that, when the mind abides unmoving and without form, it is known in its real nature of pure Consciousness. This Consciousness is Brahman. If the mind is given no quality or definition, not even the definition that it is an existent entity, the one Reality, Brahman, shines self-revealed, and the conclusive, irrefutable experience is that Brahman alone is the identity of the Self.

The destruction of the illusory modifications of the mind, manifesting as misidentifications and attachments, is the meditation that results in experience of the Self. The disciple, eager to know the extent of the freedom bestowed by the instruction already imparted by the glorious guru, requests to know if the experience of the Self is reserved to states of meditation and samadhi, in which there is no functioning of the body, senses, etc., or if it prevails when these instruments of action and cognition, inclusive of the mind, are caused to engage in the various functions that they must perform or undergo by virtue of the effect of prarabdha karma—the karma that is the cause of the present life's manifest experience.

Liberation is attained when the seeker realizes that there has been no bondage, there is no bondage, and there will not be any bondage for the Self, utterly devoid of an ego. The Self ever is as it is. Time, space, the world, activities, and all else neither affect it nor stand apart from it. Wherever and whenever, with whatever and however, the Self, pure Being, is as it is. Its bliss is inseparable from it; likewise its freedom. In order to be liberated and blissful, one must realize the Self to be always free from the body, senses, prana, mind, etc. This freedom, the result of inquiring into the true nature of the Self, is not dependent on the states of activity and inactivity of those very things that it transcends.

Answering every question and doubt, Sri Ramana, the wondrous guru who unfailingly liberates all his disciples and devotees and reveals the Truth of the Self in their hearts, dissolves the doubt raised at its very root. Only such a sadguru can do so, causing bliss and peace to pervade the entirety of the disciples' experiences. Those who have found refuge in his grace are never forsaken, but, following His instruction precisely, they are undoubtedly liberated from all of the imagined bondage—the dreaded samsara, the repetitive cycle of illusion with its birth and death—to abide in immortal Bliss.

As by analogy and parable essential spiritual wisdom can be easily assimilated, using physical representations for that which is not physical but purely spiritual, Sri Bhagavan masterfully gives the example of the man engaged as an actor in a drama. The character he plays is a fiction, and he knows that. He knows that he is not what appears to be. He is not truly engaged in the activities of the character, and, within himself, he has no attachment whatsoever to what is occurring in the drama. He is dispassionate, even when his face and limbs are called upon to display emotion. He knows that the drama, inclusive of the scene and the characters, is entirely unreal.

So it is with one who abides in the firm conviction of the Truth of the Self. He knows that the world is unreal, that he is not what appears, that he is not a character in samsara, that he is not a body, and that he truly does absolutely nothing, for he is the unmoving, formless, Self.

Activities of the body are not at all a cause of the ignorant conception of "I am the body." Ignorance does not have an outer cause. It is conjured up from oneself, and one is free to accept or reject it. If you yourself do not conjure up ignorance, nothing else will do so for you.

Ignorance does not come from an external source, be it the world, the body, or the body's activities. Ignorance does not come from within, for "within" is the Self, of the nature of infinite Wisdom and Bliss. It does not come from anything in between, for "between" (the knot of the heart, the mind, or the ego) is only an effect of ignorance, something imagined within ignorance. And ignorance cannot come from itself, for such a view would be based upon its pre-existence to do so, which is absurd. So, from where does ignorance come? The Maharshi has revealed it: see for whom the ignorance appears and realize that it has not come and only the Self is.

The natural state of the mind is absorption in nondual Consciousness. Should the mind stray from its natural state into the realm of delusion, which is contained within itself, the remedy for such is Self-inquiry. One should immediately inquire, for there is never a good time to be deluded and to suffer. Always is the time to be blissfully wise. One should immediately negate any misidentification with the body and inquire, "Who am I?" to realize the Truth of the Self and thus reinstate the mind in the natural state. The natural state is the pure state, the state of Consciousness not mingled with any notion or dualism.

The inquiry into the Self should be constant. It should be pursued one-pointedly with full faith in its efficacy. By the power of inquiry, one is liberated from all the delusions regarding one's own existence. Let there be this inquiry, "Who am I?" the moment that delusion appears, and that delusion will be extinguished there and then. If the inquiry were practiced uninterruptedly, illusion could not even appear. The inquiry should be practiced as intensely as one wants to be happy and at peace.

All suffering is due solely to ignorance. Ignorance is destroyed by Knowledge just as darkness vanishes with the advent of light. That all-illusion-destroying Knowledge, Self-Knowledge, is the power of Siva. It is realized by Self-inquiry. With ignorance destroyed, leaving not the least trace of differentiation, the innate Bliss of the Self remains, unobscured, uncaused, and imperishable. It is supreme peace, the quiescence of Siva's own nature. Siva destroys the nonexistent illusions and remains as the residuum of nondual Absolute Being. It is in That that the mind of the bhakta or the yogi or the jnani is dissolved and remains quiescent. The Self shines self-resplendent without hindrance.

Upon such realization, one sees that all activity, manifestation, sensations, and phenomena are without any power to bind one or interrupt the experience of meditation. The essence of meditation is perpetual.

As for the world, one who is unattached to it, having discerned its transitory nature and having understood that the eternal source of bliss is within, comprehends its dream-like nature. Like a dream, this world is unreal and of no actual substance. Like a dream, this world appears to be perceived by senses, which are also dreamlike and illusory. As in a dream, this world appears as if external when, in fact, it is but a hallucination within one's own mind. As with a dream, this world is composed of the state of mind that perceives it. Like a dream, this world is transitory. As with a dream, the only thing real about it is the Consciousness that pervades it but is invisible within it, as Consciousness is free of all form. One who knows the dream-like nature of the world awakens from it and realizes the Reality of the Self, Brahman.

By grace and inquiry into the Self, one finds the direct experience of the Self. It is "plenary," that is, full and absolute. The Self is the perfect fullness and, being One without a second, is absolute. Misidentification and its consequent attachment are called forgetfulness of the Self. Freedom from misidentification and attachment is remembrance of the Self. Bhakti (devotion) is complete surrender unto That, which is God, which is Guru, and which, indeed, is the Self. Supreme bhakti is remaining unwaveringly surrendered so that neither the notion "I" nor any other notion obscures the experience of That. Yoga is union with That, the merger of the mind with That. Such yoga controls the delusions of the mind by eliminating their root—the notion of a separate mind. There is thus no scope for the mind's vagaries, and the experience of the Self is unobstructed. Jnana is Knowledge of the Self, the one Reality. It signifies remaining free of all misidentification so that neither the notion "I," nor of a "mind," nor of anything else arises. It is the

Knowledge in which knowing and Being are one and the same. It is the discernment that the Reality ever alone is and the unreal has never come to be. It is the experience of one's own Self, in which all duality has been effaced. All other fiery spiritual practices intensely performed—tapas— should be understood in the same way.

This is the Truth revealed and the path shown by all the enlightened sages, the rishi-s, who are full with the limitless Wisdom and Bliss. With grace, they have compassionately revealed the teaching, preserving it with their own experience. The state of such sages defies description. All who have sought to know it have disappeared never to return, like rivers in the ocean, and dwell as one with them, like the many "trees" of a banyan forest.

The great sage, the Maharshi, reveals the Truth of the Self with illimitable grace and supreme Knowledge. He is Siva, the Self. He is Brahman. His word is the word of Siva. His silence is the silence of Brahman. All who absorb his precious instruction and inquire into the Self are exquisitely blessed. They awaken from the dream of the world, abide nonattached to all, dwell in sublime peace, are unmoved by anything whatsoever, are the same in activity and inactivity, and, attaining the supreme Realization of the eternal Self, the one Reality, abide in infinite Wisdom and Bliss.

Om Sri Ramanarpanamastu

Om May this be an offering to Sri Ramana

13

Disciple: When there is activity in regard to works, we are neither the agents of those works nor their enjoyers. The activity is of the three instruments (i.e., the mind, speech, and body). Could we remain (unattached) thinking thus?

The Maharshi: After the mind has been made to stay in the Self, which is its Deity, and has been rendered indifferent to empirical matters because it does not stray from the Self, how can the mind think as mentioned above? Do not such thoughts constitute bondage? When such thoughts arise due to residual impressions (vasana-s), one should restrain the mind from flowing that way, endeavor to retain it in the Self-state, and make it turn indifferent to empirical matters.

Commentary:

Om Namo Bhagavate Sri Ramanaya

The Self is ever unmoving. It is free from individuality, free from the mind, and free from the body. Bodiless, it is not the performer of any action. Without a mind, it does not experience, enjoy, or reap the fruits of any action. All the illusory activities are conducted by the illusory instruments of the body, organs of speech, and the mind. The guna-s are busy with the guna-s, the elements with the elements. If one knows that all manifestation is within the mind, the mind is busy with itself. The Self is ever transcendent, still, and at peace. It is unattached, innately.

The disciple desires to know if detachment can be gained by thinking about the activities of these instruments as belonging to them and not to the Self. Is it possible to dwell constantly with this thought?

The Maharshi's Wisdom transcends all—even the most sublime thoughts. It is realized by grace and absorption in the Self. If the mind stays in the Self, it is no longer a mind for all that remains is the Reality of pure, indivisible Consciousness. The Self is the God and Lord of the mind. If the mind offers itself to this Supreme Lord, Bliss-Consciousness shines uninterruptedly. When all notions are known as unreal, the mind stays in the Self. When misidentification ceases, the mind stays in the Self. When one inquires constantly into the Self, the mind stays there, and all duality vanishes.

The mind that stays in the Self is permeated by Bliss. It has ceased to conceive of anything, including itself. It does not think of dualistic, ignorant notions. It does not think of nondual, wise ideas. It does not exist; Consciousness alone is. How can that which does not exist think or create notions? How can that which is pure Bliss stray toward or become attached to anything whatsoever? If there is no trace of attachment, who requires such thoughts or methods?

63

Notions of any kind are bondage. Bondage is illusory. The Self is neither a notion of attachment nor detachment. It is always as it is. To imagine otherwise is delusion, and such alone is the only bondage.

Ignorance has no self-existence. It is constituted merely of conceptual tendencies (vasana-s). The state free of vasana-s is the true and natural one. One should abide with utter indifference—without the least vasana of attachment—toward the world. The world is unreal. To abide in the Knowledge of Reality, one must be free of all that is unreal. Whenever a vasana appears, it should be destroyed there and then by inquiring into the Reality of the Self and thus dissolve the differentiated mind into the natural state—the formless Absolute.

Have no attachment to the transitory matter of this dream-like world. Have neither desire nor aversion toward it, but know it to be unreal like a mirage. Be unmoving in the Self, which is worldless.

Sri Bhagavan awakens one from the dream of this world and causes one to dwell in the Knowledge of the Self. His grace, incomprehensible to the mind, is quite beyond anything of the world. His Wisdom is completely liberating, revealing the infinite, formless, nature of the Self. Whoever approaches him with a heart full of devotion, intensely following his instruction to inquire into the Self, finds that the world and attachment have vanished, and, with the mind forever dissolved in That, abides in infinite Wisdom and Bliss.

Om Sri Ramanarpanamastu
Om May this be an offering to Sri Ramana

13

(continued)

The Maharshi: One should not give room in the mind for such thoughts as: "Is this good? Or, is that good? Can this be done? Or, can that be done?" One should be vigilant even before such thoughts arise and make the mind stay in its native state. If any little room is given, such a (disturbed) mind will do harm to us while posing as our friend; like the foe appearing to be a friend, it will topple us down. Is it not because one forgets one's Self that such thoughts arise and cause more and more evil? While it is true that to think through discrimination, "I do not do anything; all actions are performed by the instruments," is a means to prevent the mind from flowing along through vasana-s, does it not also follow that only if the mind flows along thought vasana-s that it must be restrained through discrimination as stated before? Can the mind that remains in the Self-state think as "I" and as "I behave empirically thus and thus"? In all manner of ways possible, one should endeavor gradually not to forget one's (true) Self, which is God. If that is accomplished, all will be accomplished. The mind should not be directed to any other matter. Even though one may perform, like a mad person, the actions that are the result of prarabdha-karma, one should retain the mind in the Self-state without letting the thought "I do" arise. Have not countless bhakta-s performed their numerous empirical functions with an attitude of indifference?

Commentary:

Om Namo Bhagavate Sri Ramanaya

The mind in delusion creates the samsara. Samsara appears by it and in it. The delusion, and hence the entire samsara, is composed purely of imagination. By the grace and Truth revealed by the guru, for whoever abides without imagination, the delusion is destroyed, and, with it, vanishes the entire samsara.

Once the reality of the Self, of the nature of Being-Consciousness, is projected on the notion of something existent other than the Self, which then appears as the illusion of a world, and the Self is misidentified with a body, the superimposition of Bliss, which is also of the Self, occurs through delusion. It is then that one is caught in the anxiety of anticipations and fears, frantically desiring to find the veiled Bliss in the things and conditions of this dream-like world-illusion. One wonders, "Is this good? Is that good? Will this bring what is good? Will that bring what is good? Will this bring me happiness? Will that prevent my happiness?" etc.

The attempt to determine what is good is an attempt to determine what will provide for one's happiness. Happiness, though, is not to be found in the objects and circumstances of the world. Happiness is within, and within is the Self. Happiness is the Self, and the Self alone is capable of direct experience of its own nature. The transitory, unreal phenomena, of an external, illusory world cannot provide the eternal, real Bliss, which is of the very nature of the Self. All the wise agree that one should abide without the least attachment to the world in order to abide in the blissful Self. Attachment is only false notions within the mind. Therefore, the Maharshi proclaims the teaching that one should remain without so much as an idea of such attachment. There should be not the least bit of room; that is, by virtue of the Wisdom revealed by Sri Bhagavan, there should not exist even the possibility of conceiving of such delusion.

By misidentifying with the body, one regards its birth, growth, decay, and death as belonging to the Self, much like a person falsely conceiving of a clear piece of crystal or glass as endowed with the colors of whatever is held near it. Harboring the "I-am-the-body" notion, one regards the activities of the body as belonging to oneself, like a person sitting on the bank of a river falsely concluding that he is moving when he observes the water moving. Such a one wonders, "Can this be done? Can that be done? I desire to do this; I desire to avoid doing that. I can do this; I cannot do that;" etc. The "I-am-the-body" notion thus manifests, in ignorance, as the "I-am-the-doer" notion and causes perplexity and suffering. The wise realize, "I am not the body. I never do anything. I am ever as I am. All forms, from thought to the world, have not really come to be. I am my own Bliss always, and I am ever unmoving. The body is not my definition, and its activities are not mine. The Supreme Lord, of the nature of infinite Consciousness alone creates, sustains, and destroys all. It does all, it is all, yet it is ever still and is never modified. In That, as That, I abide." Such is their sure Knowledge, even without giving rise to such thoughts.

Free from the superimposition regarding happiness and the "I am the doer" misidentification, one remains in one's true state. In practicing the teaching that unfailingly liberates one from all of the imagined bondage, bestowed by the great sage of incomparable Wisdom—the Maharshi—it is not necessary to wait until ignorance arises prior to employing the teaching. Sri Bhagavan says that one should be vigilant even before the arising of delusive notions and make the mind remain in its natural state. The mind in its natural state contains no ignorance. In its natural state, the mind has no separate form; rather, it is one with the infinite Consciousness, which is the Self. If one abides steeped in the Knowledge of the Self, with the realization of the nonexistence of the mind, there is no possibility of delusive notions, which are dependent upon the assumption of the existence of a mind, arising. Furthermore, if one is steadfast in nonattachment, even the first thought of attachment will be seen as entirely incongruous with one's real state, and immediately that notion will be destroyed by the inquiry into the Self, which is the abode of Bliss. If one abides as bodiless Being, even a single notion of embodiment or doership will be recognized as utterly false the moment it arises. When a notion is realized to have utterly nothing to do with one's identity, the reality, and happiness, it ceases to bind and ceases to exist.

The mind absorbed in the nondual Consciousness is at peace. The mind enthralled with its own imagined dualisms is perturbed. If the mind, which is but a collection of inert thoughts, is assigned the task of knowing Reality or defining the Self, it will fail. It will attempt to conjure up any number of notions, but these, far from revealing the real Self, only serve to obscure the Truth. Obscuration of the Truth is delusion; delusion alone is the cause of bondage and suffering. Ignorance of the Self is suffering and bondage. Self-Knowledge is Bliss and Liberation. Therefore, the wise aspirant relinquishes belief in all thought and does not mistake that foe for a friend. The wise yogi remains steadfast in the certain Knowledge of the Self and, remaining free from thought, is blissfully devoid of attachment, the notion of doership, desire and aversion, anticipation and fear—indeed, the entire illusion of samsara.

Thoughts about Self-Knowledge, inclusive of those aimed at prompting or expressing discrimination, may be useful as long as contrary thoughts of delusion are present. If one, taking the direct path to Self-Realization, does not conjure up such ignorance to begin with, where is the necessity to think such wiser thoughts? When the sun has arisen, the lamp is no longer needed, and the original face does not depend on the image in the mirror.

All activities are performed by the instruments of action and perception (karmendriya-s and jnanendriya-s). The Self, the "I," remains ever beyond action. Taking thought of this fact does not make it more so; it simply is an aid to the seeker who is still confounded with a vasana (a tendency) to conceive of the "I" as the performer of action. The Maharshi reveals that such a practice is required only if the mind pursues such a vasana. If the mind remains absorbed in pure, nondual Consciousness, the Self-state of perfect fullness and peace, even the notion "I" will not be conceived, so how will the concept of "I do" be conjured up?

You are always the Self and can never be otherwise. The difference between bliss and suffering is that between Knowledge and ignorance. Ignorance consists of misidentification, or the superimposition of notions upon the conceptless Self, of the objective on the nonobjective, form upon the formless. Knowledge is abidance as Being-Consciousness, free of misidentification or superimposition. Self-Realization is neither an event in time nor determined by time, for the Self ever is as it is. If there is ignorance regarding the nature of your own Self, you should seek to be free of it in order to regain the natural state of Bliss by any means. If the Knowledge revealed by the guru is instantly absorbed, by you being absorbed in it, there is Liberation, or Self-Realization. If there are recurring vasana-s, you should practice as revealed by Sri Bhagavan so as to destroy those vasana-s of forgetfulness of your true nature. The result, the state free of vasana-s, is Liberation, or Self-Realization. Self-Realization is the state of being That, of being God.

With the Realization of the Self, all is accomplished. The Realization is abidance as That, which leaves nothing further to be attained, no other aim to be accomplished, and no other happiness to be desired. It is abidance as That, the wisdom of which leaves nothing more to be known, the space-like freedom of which leaves no other greater freedom to be attained, the vast peace of which leaves no further peace to be secured. It is blissful immortality. It is the ineffable, immutable State. In truth, it is the only state.

Let not the mind be diverted to illusion, but, being one-pointedly turned inward, let it be dissolved in the Self. Whatever action prarabdha-karma ordains for the body, abide in the true state of the Self, free of the concepts of "I," "this," and "I do." Whatever be the appearance, let there be abidance in the certain Knowledge of the unborn, unmoving, undying Self being alone one's identity. Inwardly, let there be utter indifference to all, while the body outwardly performs its activities. This state of pure Knowledge is the very same as realized by supreme devotion (bhakti). The bhakta (devotee), surrendering all to God—or to the Sadguru—is completely divested of the illusions of "I," "mine," and "I do." The bhakta-s are completely detached from the fruits of their actions. They abide, by the power of devotion, free from the body and its limitations. By their devotion, they realize, "Nothing is mine; nothing is I. All is of the Supreme, and all occurs by the singular power of the Supreme." Being entirely absorbed in their devotion, they are blissfully detached from all else. They are one with the Lord, lost in the infinite ocean of grace. By the power of their devotion, their minds, like a burnt rope, have been rendered incapable of creating bondage. By Knowledge and by devotion, one enjoys the disembodied, completely liberated state even here and now.

Whoever, with a heart full of devotion, receives and absorbs this profound Self-Knowledge revealed by the Maharshi, remaining free of all attachment, liberates himself from the notions of "I" and "mine," the dualism of "I" and "this," and the delusion of "I do," is freed from all vasana-s and bondage, and, abiding in the natural state of the Self, for which there is no alternative and in which there is no mind, is completely absorbed in infinite Wisdom and Bliss.

14

Disciple: What is the real purpose of sannyasa (renunciation)?

The Maharshi: Sannyasa is only the renunciation of the "I"-thought and not the rejection of the external objects. He who has renounced (the "I"-thought) thus remains the same whether he is alone or in the midst of the extensive samsara. Just as when the mind is concentrated on some object it does not observe other things even though they may be proximate, so also, although the sage may perform any number of empirical acts, in reality he performs nothing, because he makes the mind rest in the Self without letting the "I"-thought arise. Even as in a dream one appears to fall head downward while in reality one is unmoving, so also the ignorant person, i.e., the person for whom the "I"-thought has not ceased, although he remains alone in constant meditation, is in fact one who performs all empirical actions. Thus the wise ones have said.

Commentary:
Om Namo Bhagavate Sri Ramanaya

Freedom from all bondage is the glory of renunciation. Complete transcendence of the world is the glory of renunciation. Steadiness beyond the pairs of opposites is the glory of renunciation. The sannyasin (one who is renounced) is unaffected by all. The sannyasin sees the unreality of all. The supreme sannyasin knows all to be the Self and neither accepts nor rejects, desires nor has aversion toward, anything. Such a sannyasin with such renunciation, who is clad only in space-like Consciousness and has neither body nor any color garment, is the wondrous guru, Bhagavan Sri Ramana Maharshi.

Some conceive of renunciation as doing with fewer external objects as one's possessions than others. Some conceive of renunciation as the assuming of certain vows, receiving initiation, and the donning of the appropriate colored robe. Some seek to know: "What is truly renunciation, and what is its purpose? What is this renunciation proclaimed by the scriptures and sages as being so essential for Liberation?" It is with this inquisitive state of mind that the disciple posed this question about the real purpose of renunciation.

The great sage, the Maharshi, whose state is inconceivable yet made realizable by his grace and teaching, declares the very essence of renunciation, which brings Liberation from all the dream-like illusion filled with innumerable, unreal fetters. It is renunciation of the "I"-notion, the ego. If the ego appears, there is illusion and ignorance, even if one has given up all but the barest necessities of bodily survival. If the ego is realized to be nonexistent, there is no illusion and no ignorance, regardless of bodily interaction with various phenomenal objects. In Sri Bhagavan's reply, "samsara" should be understood to refer to phenomenal activities such as family life, etc., and not in the sense of the repetitive cycle of birth and death, for it is well-known that he who has realized the Self, and is thus free of the ego, is the unborn and imperishable Brahman and has neither death nor rebirth— nor does he see any illusion.

The abandonment of objects must be accompanied by detachment from them if such renunciation is to be truly effective. Indeed, most aspirants will physically renounce something upon pursuit of Self-Realization; not every activity and every possession will remain the same as before. The detachment, though, is the essence. Whether one carries on with many activities or with very few, with many objects around or with few—or at least the few for which one is responsible—the detachment must be complete. Attachment is bondage due to the projection of happiness upon unreal objects of an unreal world. Detachment is Liberation due to Knowledge of the Self, which is Bliss and the sole-existent Reality.

The unity of detachment and Knowledge is expressed in *Who am I?* by the Maharshi, "Not to desire anything extraneous to oneself constitutes vairagya (dispassion) or nirasa (desirelessness). Not to give up one's hold on the Self constitutes Jnana (Knowledge). But really, vairagya and Jnana are one and the same. Just as the pearl diver, tying stones to his waist, dives down into the depths and gets the pearl from the sea-bed, even so, every aspirant, pledged to vairagya, can dive deep into himself and realize the precious Atman. If the earnest seeker would only cultivate 'remembrance' (smrti) of the true nature of the Self until he has realized it, that alone would suffice."

The Maharshi reveals that the true sannyasa, or renunciation, is the abandonment of the ego-notion. If the ego is rejected, all has been renounced, regardless of the state of the body. This very same point is elucidated at length by Vasishtha in the story of Cudala and Sikhidhvaja. Though the ancient scripture of Yoga Vasishtha is not mentioned by name at this point in *Self-Inquiry,* the Maharshi did frequently refer to its teachings and stories, inclusive of that of Cudala, in which this emphasis on renunciation of the ego is identical. To express or to prompt this egolessness is the actual purpose of any external representation of renunciation.

He who is free of the "I"-notion is ever the same. Whether in solitude or in a crowd, active or still, he abides in the Self and revels in his own Bliss. He sees the Reality clearly. He knows that it is only an unreal body performing unreal actions in unreal relation to unreal objects of an unreal world. He is at peace and remains undismayed by the appearance and disappearance of things.

When your mind is concentrated upon some object, it has no concern with other things to the point that even nearby objects are not noticed. This is analogous to the sage whose body is engaged in activities, yet who unswervingly abides in the Truth of "no-creation." "He makes his mind rest in the Self;" that is, his mind is in the natural, effortless state of absorption in the Self. He has turned it completely inward so that it has dissolved its apparent separate existence to be ever merged with the Absolute Consciousness, which is its real nature. He does not let the "I"-thought arise; that is, he does not imagine the ego, or separate individuality, and has found that it has no self-sustaining capacity. With no ego, there is no mind; with no mind, there is no dualism; with no dualism, there is no illusion or bondage. Such is the state of him who has truly renounced. For such a one, renunciation is innate, for his identity is solely that of the infinite, eternal Self, which, being ever free and One without a second, being alone existent and the only Existence everywhere and at all times, is ever detached, or renounced, completely.

In a dream, one may imagine ever so many events. One may imagine that he is falling headfirst into an abyss, yet all the while he is comfortably reclining on a bed. There is no actual motion, though in the dream it seems otherwise. So it is when one, in ignorance, misidentifies the Self as an ego and with a body. Then, even when seated still in meditation, one is moving—whirling—in the vortices of illusion. One is thus still engaged in "empirical actions" of all sorts. Indeed, all action arises after such misidentification, and one who is engaged in misidentification can thus be said to be doing all things. It is like the case of the person who is dreaming. His own dreaming mind is producing all things and their interactions.

The wise, though, beholding the luminous Truth revealed by the guru, inquire and know the Self as it is. Free of misidentification, they abide as the unmoving one. They remain awake and do not dream of illusion. Their peace is unperturbed, and their happiness is full. With little or with a lot, they remain contented in the Self. The greatest treasure is theirs by the grace of the guru. They have nothing, yet all is theirs. They know the Self, which is not a single thing, yet is all. It is this state, space-like and free, with the darkness of delusion dispelled by the fire of wisdom and detachment, that is the renunciation that is of utmost necessity.

Sri Bhagavan ever reveals the Truth. He is the guru who shows the unreal to be nonexistent and the Reality alone to be. He has revealed what the scriptures and sages have declared to be the highest. With perfect clarity, he has shown the true meaning of renunciation. Whoever renounces, as the Maharshi has explained, and is thus without an ego "I," who by this instruction causes his mind to repose in the Self, will be completely free in activity and inactivity, whether alone or not, and, abiding in the True State, which has no "other" or "second thing," will abide in infinite Wisdom and Bliss.

Om Sri Ramanarpanamastu
Om May this be an offering to Sri Ramana

15

Disciple: The mind, sense organs, etc., have the ability to perceive; yet, why are they regarded as perceived objects?

The Maharshi:

Drik (Knower)	Drisya (Known object)
1) The seer	Pot (i.e., the seen object)
Further	
2) The eye organ	Body, pot, etc.
3) The sense of sight	The eye organ
4) The mind	The sense of sight
5) The individual soul	The mind
6) Consciousness (the Self)	The individual soul

As shown in the previous scheme, since we, the Consciousness, know all objects, we are said to be drik (knower). The categories ending with pot are the objects seen, since they are what are known. In the table of "knowledge: ignorance (i.e., knower-known)," given above, among the knowers and objects of knowledge, it is seen that one is knower in relation to another; yet, since that one is object in relation to another, none of these categories is, in reality, the knower. Although we are said to be the "knower" because we know all, and not the "known" because we are not known by anything else, we are said to be the "knower" only in relation to the known objects. In truth, however, what is called the "known" is not apart from us. And so we are the Reality that transcends those two (the knower and the known). All the others fall within the knower-known categories.

Commentary:

Om Namo Bhagavate Sri Ramanaya

The great sage who sees the Truth is the Truth himself. With the infinite eye of pure Consciousness, he sees that which is indivisible and infinite, which transcends noumenon and phenomena, and which is the Self of all. To that great sage, the Maharshi, Sri Ramana who delights the heart with the blissful, perfect fullness, we offer our salutations and our unending gratitude.

The Self, of the nature of unalloyed Consciousness, is the Light of all lights. It is one and nondual. It is, indeed, Knowledge itself. Of this entire universe, it is the solitary knower. Nothing objective, be it gross or subtle, is endowed with Consciousness, and Consciousness, itself, never becomes an object.

Ignorance, manifesting as superimposition, confounds Consciousness with what is objective, and one's Being is thereby misidentified with those objective things. In spiritual practice, one should diligently extricate the Self from these misidentifications, eliminating the superimposed objective forms from pure Consciousness. We are the knower and can never be an object of knowledge. What are mistaken to be the knower, such as the individual, the mind, the senses, or the sense organs, are actually only the known, with each one that is more subtle appearing as if the knower in relation to that which is grosser. Inquiring, one realizes that what is objective is not the Self and is unreal. Reality, which is the Self, is of the nature of true Knowledge, which is formless Consciousness. What is unreal is only ignorance. In Reality, there is no "unreal," duality being nonexistent. The nonobjective Reality of pure Consciousness alone exists. It is the nondual Self.

The Self is the unknown knower of all that is known. It is the only knower. Nothing else has the capacity to know, whether correctly or incorrectly, and, therefore, nothing can supplant that Consciousness.

Sri Bhagavan, the perfect sadguru, draws one to abide as the knower, transcendent of all objective definition and form. That knower is formless and thus infinite. It is without limit and is eternal. All of the known is known by and in the knower. Nothing known can exist apart from the knower. The universe appears only in the Self and cannot exist apart from the Self. There is, then, actually no known but only the knower. The Self is called the knower only in relation to the known. As there is no known, the Self is, in highest truth revealed by the Maharshi, not to be defined as a knower. The nondual Self is neither a knower nor the known but is all-transcendent. Thus, in Gambhiram Seshayya's original notebook, Sri Bhagavan wrote, "Thus we are the seer and all are the seen, but as the seen does not exist apart from the seer, we are both the seer and the seen and that which transcends both."

Whoever abides as the transcendent Reality of the nature of nondual Consciousness, having keenly inquired into the nature of the knower and disidentified from all that is known, is liberated from ignorance and, by the grace of the guru, realizes the Self to thus abide in infinite Wisdom and Bliss.

Om Sri Ramanarpanamastu
Om May this be an offering to Sri Ramana

16

Disciple: How do egoity, soul, self, and Brahman come to be identified?

The Maharshi:

The Example	*The Exemplified*
1) The iron-ball	Egoity
2) The heated iron-ball	The soul which appears as a superimposition on the Self
3) The fire that is in the heated iron-ball	The Light of Consciousness, i.e., the immutable Brahman, which shines in the soul in every body
4) The flame of the fire which remains as one	The all-pervading Brahman which remains as one

From the example previously given, it will be clear how egoity, soul, witness, and All-witness come to be identified.

Commentary:

Om Namo Bhagavate Sri Ramanaya

In the form of a table, the initial portion of the Maharshi's wisdom-permeated answer is presented. It is a display of an analogy in which a heated ball of iron represents the experience of individuality and Brahman.

The iron ball is said to be the ego, which is something completely inert, possessing nothing of Consciousness whatsoever. It is merely a notion and is usually identified with the forms of the body and mind. When pervaded by Consciousness, that is, when it is superimposed upon Consciousness, which is the Self, it appears as if a sentient being, a "soul," which is represented as a heated iron ball. The heat is the awareness of a sentient being, which in truth belongs to Consciousness alone and is in no way an attribute of the ego.

Represented by the element of fire, which appears as the aforementioned heat, is the Light of Consciousness. That Consciousness is Brahman, the vast Absolute, which shines as the innermost essence of every being. Immutability is its nature. It is subject to neither birth nor death, cannot be conditioned or modified, and is innately free of limit and form. It is the Reality, which ever is as it is. Therefore, even defining it in relation to form, as the pervader or indweller, is not the final truth. Represented by the indivisible element of fire is Brahman, which is nondual. It is said to be "all-pervading." It permeates all without exception. It suffuses the sentient and the insentient. It pervades the world; it pervades the mind. Nothing divides it, and there is not anything separate from it. If this description is understood conclusively, no separate "all" remains to be pervaded, as Brahman is the pervader, the pervaded, and the pervading entirely. It is undifferentiated.

The Light or Consciousness, which knows in a nonattached manner the soul or mind, is the witness. When the same is realized as the infinite Self, before which all minds

77

rise and fall, in which universe upon universe appears and disappears, it is referred to as the "All-witness."

Sri Bhagavan, in his graciousness and with his thorough-knowing Wisdom, continues to explain this knowledge to the disciple:

The Maharshi: Just as in the wax-lump that is with the smith, numerous and varied metal particles lie included and all of them appear to be one wax-lump, so also in deep sleep the gross and subtle bodies of all the individual souls are included in the cosmic maya, which is nescience, of the nature of sheer darkness, and, since the souls are resolved in the Self, becoming one with it, they see everywhere darkness alone. From the darkness of sleep, the subtle body, viz. egoity, and from that (egoity), the gross body arise respectively. Even as the egoity arises, it appears superimposed on the nature of the Self, like the heated iron ball. Thus, without the soul (jiva), which is the mind or egoity that is conjoined with the Consciousness-Light, there is no witness of the soul, viz. the Self, and without the Self, there is no Brahman that is the All-witness. Just as when the iron ball is beaten into various shapes by the smith, the fire that is in it does not change thereby in any manner, even so the soul may be involved in ever so many experiences and undergo pleasures and pains, and yet the Self-Light that is in it does not change in the least thereby, and, like the ether, it is the all-pervasive pure Knowledge that is one, and it shines in the heart as Brahman.

Commentary:
The state of deep sleep is regarded as causal in nature, for in it the manifestations, gross and subtle, appearing as all that is experienced in waking and dream, are resolved temporarily only to spring forth again. Within deep sleep, dreams appear, one of which is the waking state. From the causal arises the subtle, which in turn manifests as the gross. All individuals, with all manifestations and permutations, are only of maya, illusion, which is of cosmic dimension.

To regard the states such as deep sleep as individualized when individuality is absent therein is false. It is only from the body-misidentified position of the ego that one assumes the descriptions of cosmic maya and one's own illusion, as well as the Self and one's own self, are different.

All of maya is only ignorance. Ignorance is sheer darkness, possessing no Consciousness of its own. Darkness is only the apparent absence of light, Knowledge, which is of the very nature of Consciousness, and is not an entity or power of its own.

From the nescient position of the individual, the Light of the Self appears as if darkness, for the individual retains no existence in that Self. For the sages who have realized the Truth, the Self is always one, the ever-existent Brahman, and darkness is impossible.

The ego and all its forms are mere superimpositions upon the real Self. The real Self is only Brahman, formless, egoless, space-like Being. All the designations and descriptions aforementioned in the context of the heated iron ball analogy are in the course of explanation for the benefit of the disciple. Thus, the "witness of the soul" is spoken of only in relation to the assumption of the existence of a soul. Likewise is it with the other explanations, inclusive of the description of Brahman as the witness of all. If that which is objective, or endowed with form, is realized to be unreal, Brahman, or the true Self, is conceived in no way whatsoever, not even as a witness, but is clearly known as it is, transcendent of all definition.

The individuals, with their experiences, are transitory, insubstantial mirages. The Self, of the nature of pure Consciousness, is never born as an individual. Whatever be the experiences of the individual, its pleasures and pains etc., the Self remains unassociated with them and unaffected by them. Like space, the Self is unmoved and unstained. Like a sun ever shining, it is undiminished and without a shadow. Whatever be the condition of the body, the senses, and prana, it is ever the same. Whatever be the dreams of the mind, it remains transcendent, as the silent, unmoving witness. It shines in the heart, that is, one's essential Being, as Brahman. It is pure Knowledge, in which ignorance can never be. Like space, it is omnipresent, free of form, all-pervading, and indivisible.

In the original notebook of Gambhiram Seshayya, this section contains two additional statements: "The universe is only an idea. It is the Heart that takes all these forms. It is the light of the Atman that shines in everybody. Hence, it is called sakshi (the witness) or turiya (the real) [literally, the fourth], wherein no ego or sense of personality remains;" and "If the mind is subdued, everything is conquered." Herein, Sri Bhagavan reveals that the entire realm of objective experience is only imagined, just as an idea is Consciousness plus imagined objectivity. He then reveals that it is only the one essential Existence, the Heart, that is all this. There is never any other. The sole power and substance, even in illusion, is only the Self, and the Self alone, thus, exists always. This Existence, which is all, is the Consciousness in everyone. Consciousness is formless and egoless. So, just as one Existence appears as all this, while ever remaining as its unformed, unborn Self, so Consciousness appears as the awareness within all, while ever remaining utterly impersonal and non-individualized. The Witness of all, the Self is undefined by anything. This Being-Consciousness is referred to as the "Fourth" in *Mandukya Upanishad,* Gaudapada's *Karika* (1:10 – 1:18 are specific to the Maharshi's instructions in this respect), Sankara's commentary thereon, in the *Ribhu Gita,* and in other Vedantic scriptures, for the Self is truly transcendent of all states of mind and their contents, as in waking and dream, and the absence of content, as in deep sleep. Therefore, what is perceived as the universe, is inwardly known as the Heart, shines as that which knows in all, is the silent witness of all, is transcendent of all states of mind, and in which there is neither ego nor the personality (consisting of the manifest vasana-s of the ego) is alone to be realized as the Self. Self-inquiry destroys the mind's imagination of differentiation and thereby yields transcendence of all. One who thus inquires knows himself to be all and to be without even a trace of "all."

By ignorance, all that is mentioned by the disciple is identified as differentiated. By the supreme Knowledge revealed by the Maharshi, differentiation is realized as nonexistent, and the true identity, which is forever nondual, alone remains. All who abandon the unreal maya to abide in true Knowledge are released from the bondage of duality and all states of nescience, and, by dwelling in divine grace, the very presence of the guru, they are absorbed in Brahman and thus abide in infinite Wisdom and Bliss.

Om Sri Ramanarpanamastu

Om May this be an offering to Sri Ramana

17

Disciple: How is one to know that in the heart the Self itself shines as Brahman?

The Maharshi: Just as the elemental ether within the flame of a lamp is known to fill without any difference and without any limit both the inside and the outside of the flame, so also the knowledge-ether that is within the Self-light in the heart fills without any difference and without any limit both the inside and the outside of that Self-light. This is what is referred to as Brahman.

Commentary:

Om Namo Bhagavate Sri Ramanaya

Sri Bhagavan has declared that the Self that shines in the heart is Brahman. It is the declaration of Brahman itself, as the guru is none other than Brahman. He is the indweller of the Heart, the inner Lord, and the Self itself. He is beyond all doubt, just as Brahman, or the Self, is beyond all doubt. There can be no discussion or contention regarding the truth of his instruction. The disciple's only concern is how to realize how true the Truth revealed is. For those who seek the Realization of the Supreme Truth, it is imperative that they not attempt to delusively interpret the Maharshi's teachings in a limited manner that would correlate to the imagination within their own minds, but rather to relinquish such limitations of the mind and, abandoning delusion, comprehend the sacred, liberating instructions in the manner of direct experience. Hence the question, "How is one to know that in the heart the Self itself shines as Brahman?"

The Maharshi immediately reveals the utter absence of difference between Brahman and the Self. The Self is of the nature of pure Consciousness. Because it illumines, or knows, all, it is referred to in terms of light. Within the heart, which is one's innermost Being, it abides and shines. If any individuality, even so much as a "knower," is attributed to it, realize that it is the all-pervading, space-like Brahman that is within and without that knower. As space has no limit, so it is with Brahman. As there are really no divisions in space, so it is with Brahman.

The Knowledge-space is the space of Consciousness. This space of Consciousness pervades the known and the unknown. It pervades the subject and the object. It is both within and without the "flame" of awareness, which owes its light to that same space of Consciousness. The space of Consciousness is utterly undifferentiated.

The differenceless Reality is revealed by the wondrous guru. Whoever comprehends this essential Knowledge finds illimitable Bliss, for the undivided is Bliss itself. Whoever, by his grace, realizes the undivided nature of Brahman and realizes that Brahman is the Self, which alone is, is liberated from all differences and limits, and, shining as Brahman itself, abides in infinite Wisdom and Bliss.

Om Sri Ramanarpanamastu
Om May this be an offering to Sri Ramana

18

Disciple: How do the three states of experience, the three bodies, etc., which are imaginations, appear in the Self-light, which is one, impartite, and self-luminous? Even if they should appear, how is one to know that the Self alone remains ever unmoving?

The Maharshi: (See diagram on following page) The Self which is the lamp (1) shines of its own accord in the inner chamber, i.e., the causal body (7) that is endowed with nescience as the inner wall (4) and sleep as the door (2); when by the vital principle as conditioned by time, karma, etc., the sleep-door is opened, there occurs a reflection of the Self in the egoity-mirror (5) that is placed next to the doorstep—Mahat-tattva (3); the egoity-mirror thus illumines the middle chamber, i.e., the dream state (8), and, through the windows which are the five cognitive sense-organs (6), the outer court, i.e., the waking state (9). When, again, by the vital principle as conditioned by time, karma, etc., the sleep-door gets shut, the egoity ceases along with waking and dream, and the Self alone ever shines. The example just given explains how the Self is unmoving, how there is difference between the Self and the egoity, and how the three states of experience, the three bodies, etc., appear.

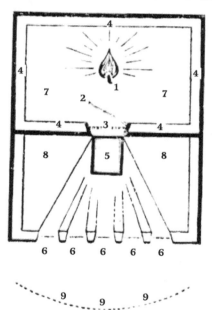

The Example	The Exemplified
(1) The lamp	The Self
(2) The door	Sleep
(3) The door-step	Mahat-tattva
(4) The inner wall	Nescience or the causal body
(5) The mirror	The egoity
(6) The windows	The five cognitive sense-organs

(7) The inner chamber   Deep sleep in which the causal body is manifest

(8) The middle chamber   Dream in which the subtle body is manifest

(9) The outer court   Waking state in which the gross body is manifest

Commentary:

Om Namo Bhagavate Sri Ramanaya

The Truth revealed by the enlightened guru is that before which all words and thoughts turn back, unable to grasp. No form of thought or expression can give definition to the formless. Out of the infinity of his grace, from Silence, he brings forth the teaching. Out of the limitlessness of his compassion, he further brings forth explanations in analogies, in images comprehensible by the mind that finds itself incapable of grasping the sacred utterances of the teaching devoid of images. The mind of the disciple advances by profound meditation from the analogy to the significance, which is the teaching, to the direct experience of the Truth of the Self.

The disciple has posed the question about the three states of waking, dream, and deep sleep, the three bodies of gross, subtle, and causal—which may be understood as corresponding to the three forms of the experiencers of the aforementioned states—and "etc.," which signifies all the tattvas, the factors constituting all experience appearing within those states. Sri Bhagavan has already shown that the Self, of the nature of self-effulgent Consciousness, requires nothing else to illuminate—know or experience—itself, that the Self is void of anything else whatsoever, and that the Self is ever indivisible and nondual. He has already declared that the three states, etc., are only imagination, without the least trace of reality. The disciple's question concerns "how," that is, it already assumes that these imaginings actually come to be. The wise understand "unreal," "imagination," "illusion" to signify the utter nonexistence of anything other than the Self. Seekers may sometimes interpret the proclamations of the sages partially or within the context of a previous perspective, so that they think that that which is now declared to be unreal does, indeed, exist in some manner. The predominant aspect of the disciple's question is, assuming that the three states, etc., do come to be, how is one then to know that the Self remains ever unmoving and immutable and that it alone does so.

Whatever is truly unmoving and unchanging is real. When superimposition occurs, something mutable is conceived as changeless, something moving as unmoving. Thus, the unreal is believed to be real. Self-Realization signifies the certain Knowledge that the Self alone is real.

The analogy employed is that of a light representing pure Consciousness, the Self. It is a fuel-less lamp shining of its own accord, situated amidst chambers representing the states of mind. The inner chamber, which is that of deep sleep, or the causal state, consists merely of space but bounded by the walls of nescience, which make it a state of mind, and the door, which is the entrance into, or the experience of, sleep. Through this door, crossing over the doorstep of mahat-tattva, the first emanation of the mind by which prakriti, the primordial or most generic substance of all manifestation, will be conceived, shines the light of the Self, whenever the door is made to open by "the vital principle," the movement of which is said to be determined by karma or in the course of time or by some other factor. The movement of "the vital principle" is that which incites the motion of the mind and prana. Mahat is defined by Sri Ramana (in *Talks with Sri Ramana Maharshi)* as the projected light from absolute Consciousness, the cosmic Consciousness that comprises all, from which the ego, body, and universe manifest.

The light of the Self, passing through the doorway in and out of deep sleep, touches the ego—inert and unreal in itself, but, in illusion, counted as a factor—and the latter, with this reflected light, appears as if an experiencer, a knower, a thinker, a seer, etc. With its subtle experiences or thought, it appears with the reflected light amidst the middle chamber of the dream state. When the same is projected through the five senses, the outer court of the waking state, which comprises the entire experience of the world, appears.

Should the "sleep door" shut, the waking and dream states, the mirror of the ego, and the mahat-tattva cease, leaving the Self alone. In either case, the Self alone shines and remains where it is. It does not move, does not change, and does not become other than what it is. It is not the individual experiencer, and it, itself, does not pass in or out of any state.

By clearly discerning the difference between the Self and the ego, one realizes the unmodified Truth. By knowing how the Self does not move from state to state, one realizes its ever-unconditioned nature. The Self has no bodies and no states. It ever is as it is, utterly transcendent and forever free. It never sleeps, dreams, or wakes. It is never embodied or disembodied. Gross, subtle, and causal do not refer to it. All depend on its light; it depends on none.

By inquiring into the nature of the Self in the manner revealed by the perfect guru, the Maharshi, one realizes the ever self-luminous Self, and, abiding as that changeless, unmoving, uncaused Consciousness, awakens from all three states and, free of the ego, abides in infinite Wisdom and Bliss.

Om Sri Ramanarpanamastu
Om May this be an offering to Sri Ramana

19

Disciple: Although I have listened to the explanation of the characteristics of inquiry in such great detail, my mind has not gained even a little of peace. What is the reason for this?

The Maharshi: The reason is the absence of strength or one-pointedness of the mind.

Commentary:
Om Namo Bhagavate Sri Ramanaya

The inquiry into the Self is the most excellent of practices. The inquiry into the Self is the most direct of paths. The inquiry into the Self is the means for the most immediate revelation of the Self. The fruit of the inquiry into the Self is supreme Bliss.

By whatever means one attempts to realize the Self, in the end one must know oneself. How is it possible to know oneself without inquiring into the nature of oneself?

Self-inquiry liberates one from all of the imagined bondage. By inquiry, one knows oneself by the Self. By inquiry, the absence of the ego is revealed as self-evident. Inquiry cannot fail, as it does not presuppose the existence of any of the very illusions or dualisms that one is attempting to transcend.

Since inquiry is concerned with the Self and since the Existence of the Self is beyond doubt in all, inquiry can be practiced by all. As the Self is full and perfect, innately endowed with its own imperishable Light, which is Knowledge itself, inquiry is for all. There is no one who is incapable of inquiry into the Self, or for whom the Self is not, or who is farther away from the Self. How far can one be from one's own Existence? The Self is immediately present. Who is other than the Self? Inquiry does not depend on the body, senses, prana, thoughts—which constitute the mind—or the "I-notion," the ego, all of which may be subject to flaws or limitations. Inquiry depends on one's own Existence, and the Knowledge of that Existence is intrinsic to it. So, who is not endowed with the ability to inquire? Inquiry is like fire, before which the apparently insuperable obstacles are mere straw. Ignorance is insubstantial, so who cannot inquire and know the Self? Moreover, are there two selves, that one could be ignorant of the other? Inquiry is full in itself and requires no auxiliary methods, for all other methods involve the use or manipulation of something that is transcended by inquiry. Inquiry is the power of Siva by which the unreal is destroyed. Inquiry alone was the boon requested of the Supreme Lord by Prahlada as related by Vasishtha.

If one is instructed in the immediately accessible supreme path by the best of gurus, but fails to turn inward with a one-pointed focus, the Truth of the Self will not be known. If the Self is not known, peace is not experienced. The Self alone is immutable, as stated earlier, and the immutable alone yields imperturbable peace. Peace is of the

Self; the Self must be known for peace. One must inquire into the nature of the Self in order to know it.

At any moment, one is either inquiring into the Self, which is the Reality, or one is inquiring into, that is following, the imaginings and vagaries of the mind, which constitute the unreal. A mind caught in its own vasana-s, or tendencies, is regarded as weak by the wise. A mind devoid of vasana-s remains focused upon the Knowledge of the Self and is regarded as strong by the wise. To wallow in the unreal is weakness; to rely on the Real as one's support is true strength. The wise say that one should attain one-pointedness of mind. It signifies an absence of notions, which constitute the diffusion of ignorance, and implies absorption in that which is without duality. There should be one-pointedness in wisdom, for is there ever an opportune moment to be deluded? A mind turned inward is spiritual strength. A mind turned outward, lost in its own projections within itself, is weakness. If inquiry were practiced one-pointedly, ignorance could not even arise. Then, what appeared as the practice would be revealed as the natural, effortless state of nondual Knowledge itself.

The intense desire for Liberation yields the necessary focus, leaving one detached from and disinterested in all else. By such one-pointedness in inquiry did Nidagha realize the Truth when instructed by Ribhu. By such focus did Rama realize who he is when instructed by Vasishtha. With such one pointedness did Janaka, fully surrendered to Ashtavakra, realize the Truth when taught by the guru. With such one-pointedness upon Knowledge did Padmapada, Suresvara, and Hastamalaka realize, being taught by Adi Sankara, and, by the same one-pointedness in his deep devotion, did Totaka realize the unveiled Absolute in the presence of his guru, Sri Sankara. One-pointed was Nachiketa, and so was it with Svetaketu when he was instructed by Uddalaka. The same is so for the rishi-s—Sanaka, Sanandana, Sanat Kumara, and Sanat Sujata (said to be the mind-born sons of Brahma, their names mean: Sanaka: ancient, lasting long; Sana or Sanat Sujata: always beautiful, or ancient and well-born; Sanat Kumara: always a youth; and Sanandana-having joy)—who realized in the silence of Daksinamurti. All were one-pointed. All realized the Self, Brahman. All abide as That alone, and their peace is eternal.

Whoever, having been blessed with instruction by the guru, comprehends the ever-present nature of the Self, and one-pointedly, with the utmost intensity, meditates upon the Self, rests firmly in the Truth of the Self and, at peace, experiences this infinite Wisdom and Bliss.

Om Sri Ramanarpanamastu
Om May this be an offering to Sri Ramana

20

Disciple: What is the reason for the absence of mental strength?

The Maharshi: The means that make one qualified for inquiry are meditation, yoga, etc. One should gain proficiency in these through graded practice, and thus secure a stream of mental modes that is natural and helpful. When the mind that has in this manner become ripe listens to the present inquiry, it will at once realize its true nature, which is the Self, and remain in perfect peace, without deviating from that state. To a mind that has not become ripe, immediate realization and peace are hard to gain through listening to inquiry. Yet, if one practices the means for mind-control for some time, peace of mind can be obtained eventually.

Commentary:
Om Namo Bhagavate Sri Ramanaya

The means of sadhana through inquiry resulting in Realization of the Self have been described in detail by Sri Bhagavan. By such Realization one abides in illimitable peace. The turning of the mind inward by inquiry into the Self will bring the experience of considerable peace. A mind desirous of transcending itself, of the dissolution of its own form, is ripe. A mind that finds peace in the presence of the guru and yearns to completely experience what he reveals is ripe. A mind that is undaunted and single-pointedly adheres to the instruction of the guru is ripe. A mind that does not follow its own notions or modes is ripe. Such a mind naturally enters into Knowledge without delay when listening to the wisdom and the inquiry revealed by the guru. For a ripe mind, even while listening, simultaneously reflection (manana), profound continuous meditation (nididhyasana) and absorption in samadhi occur.

Inquiry is the formless path yielding the Realization of the formless Self. If the seeker feels that it is impossible to practice any of what has been revealed thus far by the Maharshi, it is incumbent upon the seeker to do whatever is necessary to make the mind ripe enough to practice that which directly results in Realization. Though the disciple requested to know the reason for the absence of strength of mind, Sri Bhagavan's response to him is that of a directive to engage in meditation, yoga, etc., of any type that will engender a ripe mind in him. Though meditation upon the formless is best, meditation upon a form is better than none at all. Though jnana, the path of Knowledge, the essence of which is Self-inquiry, is best, better is it to pursue any form of yoga than none at all. Though the ideal state is one free of all mental modes, a stream of beneficial, spiritually inclined modes far surpasses diffusion and the random vagaries and conjurings of a mind that has neither jnana nor yoga. "Etc." in the text refers to any form of worship, contemplation, or meditation.

Whatever be the spiritual practice pursued, it should be practiced with one's utmost energy and attention. Thus, one gains proficiency with introverting the mind. Whatever be the effort or time expended on acquiring introversion of mind, such is well spent. Ripeness of mind should be attained without delay. To turn the mind outward is merely to prolong suffering and to postpone bliss. Such a mind does not inquire even when presented with the opportunity and does not retain the wise instruction even when heard repeatedly. For such a mind, the ever-present peace seems remote and the Self, though the one Reality, is not realized.

If the mind becomes ripe, it will absorb this essential Knowledge, destroy its own form or bondage by inquiry, and remain in perfect peace upon the realization of its true nature. The nature of the mind is always pure Consciousness, which is the Self. Yet the introspective mind alone realizes the truth of this. Then, from the peace of the pure Self, in which Consciousness alone is realized as the one Existence and in which there is no separate entity to be referred to as "a mind," there is no deviation.

In ignorance there is an absence of strength of mind. By adherence to the nondual Truth revealed by Sri Ramana, there is the strength of the immovable Reality and an absence of the mind.

Whoever with a ripe mind receives the precious teaching of the Maharshi, the revelation of pure Advaita Vedanta, and inquires to know the Self, abides in imperturbable peace and thus, dwelling without deviation from the Truth of the Self, realizes infinite Wisdom and Bliss.

Om Sri Ramanarpanamastu
Om May this be an offering to Sri Ramana

21

Disciple: Of the means for mind-control, which is the most important?

The Maharshi: Breath-control is the means for mind control.

Commentary:

Om Namo Bhagavate Sri Ramanaya

Dissolution of the mind comes by inquiry or by surrender. Control of mind is not to be equated with dissolution of the mind, though, as just explained, it may be beneficial for certain aspirants as preliminary to that which results in Self-Realization.

For control of mind, characterized primarily by the attribute of alert calmness, control of prana is recommended by the yogins. Prana is life energy, which, though subtle in nature, is closely associated with the breath. Control of prana can result in temporary control of the mind. Prana may be controlled either by the mind directly in meditation or by grosser means such as the regulation of the breath. In

Vivekacudamani (v. 169, v. 167 in some editions) Sri Sankara explains, "It (the sheath of the mind) manifests itself as what pervades the previous sheath (i.e., the sheath of prana)." The pervader is always subtler than the pervaded. What is subtler is more powerful; thus the mind's control over the prana. The controlled prana may, in turn, control the mind, that is, bring about the temporary abeyance of its wanderings. Though all is contained within the mind, it is a divine dispensation that some of what appears in the mind is capable of altering the mind, though how it is altered is still determined by the mind, itself.

In the original notebook of Gambhiram Seshayya, according to B. V. Narasimha Swami, a passage appears appended to chapter 33 that is said to contain the answer to a similar question asked by the disciple at another time. Though the precise time is not stated, the answer appears appropriate to the theme of this portion of *Self-inquiry* in as much as it pertains to control of the mind. It reads thus: "Forms that interfere with the main course or current of meditation should not be allowed to distract the mind. Bring yourself back into the Self, the witness, unconcerned with the distractions. That is the only way to deal with such interruptions. Never forget the Self."

"Forms that interfere" may be understood in a twofold manner. First, forms may be understood to be anything sensed, inclusive of the body. If, in relation to any such experience, one inquires as for whom they (the forms) are, the objective outlook is abandoned and the focus is upon the knower. The inquiry should proceed so that the identity is known as the knower only, the silent unaffected Witness, which is innately detached from all phenomena. Second, forms may be regarded as anything objective, inclusive of all thought. Since the world is in the mind, such thoughts may appear as abstract mental creations or as apparent sensory phenomena. Again, if the inquiry "For whom is this?" is practiced, the identity and reality are withdrawn from such distractions, and one abides as the Witness, which is of the nature of pure Consciousness. A distraction is such only due to the ignorance of misidentification. The same thought or object, devoid of any misidentification, offers no distraction at all from the essential Knowledge. Keen observation of the mind in meditation shows that a misidentification, starting with the "I" notion, must first arise for distractions in the form of other ideas or mental images to be conceived. Moreover, in the perpetually detached, formless Consciousness, which is the Self, there are no such things as thoughts, objects, and distractions. The instruction to never forget the Self is indicative of the importance of Self-inquiry and the thought-transcendent nature of Self-Knowledge.

Whoever, having mastered his mind by following the spiritual instructions of the Maharshi, who is the Master without rival, the supreme yogin, and devoted to Him who is the Lord of all minds and all prana, knows himself as the silent Witness and remains undistracted by illusion due to Knowledge of the Self, his identity absorbed in That, happily and peacefully realizes infinite Wisdom and Bliss.

Om Sri Ramanarpanamastu
Om May this be an offering to Sri Ramana

22

Disciple: How is breath to be controlled?

The Maharshi: Breath can be controlled either by absolute retention of breath (kevala-kumbhaka) or by regulation of breath (pranayama).

Commentary:

Om Namo Bhagavate Sri Ramanaya

Prana can be controlled by "absolute retention," that is retention alone, or by pranayama, i.e., regulation of the breath. The former may be understood in the grosser sense of cessation of respiratory processes or more subtly as the cessation of agitation or motion in the prana. In the latter case, the stillness of prana tends to prompt the mind toward stillness as well, and the two subside in the source and substratum of both of them. Whatever be the method employed, the goal of spiritual practice, which is the return of the mind to, and absorption in, the Self, must remain clearly in view.

Whoever abandons the outer world, with mind and prana controlled, meditates on the Truth revealed within by the guru who stands ever transcendent of all, and thus sees the infinite Light of the Self, is at peace in That which alone is, and ever rejoicing, at peace, in the wondrous grace that reveals all plainly like a fruit in the palm of one's hand, is absorbed in infinite Wisdom and Bliss.

Om Sri Ramanarpanamastu
Om May this be an offering to Sri Ramana

23

Disciple: What is absolute retention of breath?

The Maharshi: It is making the vital air stay firmly in the heart even without exhalation and inhalation. This is achieved through meditation on the vital principle, etc.

Commentary:

Om Namo Bhagavate Sri Ramanaya

This kevala-kumbhaka is achieved through meditation upon the prana even without regulation of the breathing process. The aim is to experience prana being firmly fixed in the Heart, which is the source and substratum. The Heart is neither physical nor subtle, and is not to be defined in bodily, subtle, or mental terms. It is the essence of Being.

Meditation is the essential factor in this practice. The kevala-kumbhaka is a mode of the prana. The prana, the animating life energy, is an aspect of the mind. Meditation is the power of Consciousness manifesting as the introverted mind. It returns the prana and mind to their source. That source is the Heart, which is of the nature of nonobjective Being, self-effulgent Consciousness, and uncaused Bliss. That is the Self, which is neither with a body nor without a body, neither with prana nor without, neither alive nor dead, neither with thoughts nor without them. That is the Absolute. It is this for which all seekers seek, to which all aspirants aspire, with which all yogins find union, and which all jnani-s know as their very Self.

Whoever, keeping sight of the final goal, which is Brahman, practices so that his prana and mind return to their origin, which is Brahman, by the grace and instruction of Sri Bhagavan, the Swami (Master) who is Brahman, comes to know all that need be known and experience all that need be experienced, and, with a heart full of unending devotion, abides in infinite Wisdom and Bliss.

Om Sri Ramanarpanamastu
Om May this be an offering to Sri Ramana

24

Disciple: What is regulation of breath?

The Maharshi: It is making the vital air stay firmly in the heart through exhalation, inhalation, and retention, according to the instructions given in the yoga texts.

Commentary:

Om Namo Bhagavate Sri Ramanaya

Prana can also be manipulated by regulation of the breath. The aim, though, should still be subsidence in the Heart. Directions for this kind of practice, especially the techniques to be employed, are found in certain yoga texts or can be learned from yogis who have mastered this practice. One must not lose track of the aim, though, but proceed to the prana itself, from there to the mind and then, with an inward mind, to inquiry into the Self. The inquiry will then reveal the Truth.

As much as a practice results in introversion of the mind, it is helpful. The Knowledge essence is that which is actually fruitful. To the degree that Knowledge is present in the practice, the practice is spiritually fruitful. The degree that Knowledge is present in a spiritual experience determines the height, or depth, of that experience. It is the Knowledge essence that brings the aspirant from the physical to the subtle (prana) to the mental to the infinite Consciousness, which is Knowledge itself.

Whoever, endowed with whatever practices, absorbs the teaching of the Maharshi, which shines like a never-setting sun, and, by its light, traces his way to the Self, is absorbed in it, and, having found that which is exceedingly dear by being drawn by Him who is love itself, abides in infinite Wisdom and Bliss.

Om Sri Ramanarpanamastu
Om May this be an offering to Sri Ramana

25

Disciple: How is breath-control the means for mind-control?

The Maharshi: There is no doubt that breath-control is the means for mind-control, because the mind, like breath, is a part of air, because the nature of mobility is common to both, because the place of origin is the same for both, and because when one of them is controlled the other gets controlled.

Commentary:
Om Namo Bhagavate Sri Ramanaya
Approached by the disciple perplexed about the mind, prana, and their relation, the guru, who is Lord over both mind and prana, and who abides with full Knowledge, that Bhagavan who is replete with the six qualities composing bhaga, that Bhagavan who knows creation and destruction, the arrival and departure of all beings, and knowledge (vidya) and ignorance (avidya), so that one who has found him has found the supreme answer, compassionately replies to the disciple to free him of his confusion.

Both mind and prana are endowed with mobility. Indeed, motion is their nature. If they are resolved into stillness, the unmoving, perpetually quiescent Self, the ultimate origin, remains. The mind controls prana, and prana can also control the mind. Of the two, the mind is subtler. Prana, existing within the mind, as does everything, also affects the mind. If the mind is resolved in silence, prana also is quiescent in its origin. If prana is controlled, the mind is also quieted or even brought to stillness, though the effect is temporary.

The mind, like prana, is regarded as composed of subtle elements. If air is understood as predominant in both, the commonality and mutual effects are readily comprehensible. Let air be resolved in space, and space in pure Consciousness, the immovable Absolute. In *Vivekacudamani,* v. 99, Adi Sankara explains the suksma sarira, or subtle body, to be the same as the linga sarira, having already described it in terms of karmendriya-s (organs of action), jnanendriya-s (the senses), prana, the five elements, and all the aspects of the mind. In *Sad-Vidya (Reality in Forty Verses),* verse 24, Sri Bhagavan equates this subtle body, or suksma sarira, with the mind. Sankara declares this linga sarira, or subtle body, to be composed of the five elements that have not undergone quintuplication (pancikarana). Vasishtha repeatedly describes the effects of prana upon the mind and the mind's states. As air is considered fundamental to prana, the same element, here, is regarded as the basis of the mind. The meaning is that one should trace the essence or source of the mind and prana and, transcending what is moving, abide as that which is unmoving.

In *Who am I?,* there are passages that parallel, to a considerable extent, the instructions that are contained in this present text dealing with prana, control of prana, the effects of that control, and the limitations of that control. Sri Bhagavan says, "For the subsidence of the mind, there is no other means more effective and adequate than Self-inquiry. Even though by other means the mind subsides, that is only apparently so; it will rise again. For instance, the mind subsides by the practice of prananyama (restraint and control of breath and vital forces); yet such subsidence lasts only as long as the control of the breath and vital forces continues; and when they are released, the mind also gets released and, immediately becoming externalized, wanders through the force of its subtle tendencies." He says, "The source of the mind on the one hand and of breath and vital forces on the other is one and the same," and, "Therefore, when the mind subsides, breath and vital forces also subside; and conversely, when the latter subside, the former also subside. Breath and vital forces are also described as the gross manifestation of the mind." He definitively declares, "The practice of pranayama is merely helpful in subduing the mind but cannot bring about its final extinction."

Whoever, blessed with the gracious instruction of the Maharshi, finds the origin of mind, prana, and all, and rests in peace there, abides in and as the motionless and dwells in infinite Wisdom and Bliss.

Om Sri Ramanarpanamastu
Om May this be an offering to Sri Ramana

26

Disciple: Since breath-control leads only to quiescence of the mind (manolaya) and not to its destruction (manonasa), how can it be said that breath-control is the means for inquiry which aims at the destruction of mind?

The Maharshi: The scriptures teach the means for gaining Self-realization in two modes—as the yoga with eight limbs (ashtanga-yoga) and as knowledge with eight limbs (ashtanga-jnana). By regulation of breath (pranayama) or by absolute retention thereof (kevala-kumbhaka), which is one of the limbs of yoga, the mind gets controlled. Without leaving the mind at that, if one practises the further discipline such as withdrawal of the mind from external objects (pratyahara), then at the end, Self-Realization, which is the fruit of inquiry, will surely be gained.

Commentary:

Om Namo Bhagavate Sri Ramanaya

Sri Bhagavan emphasizes again the necessity of going beyond control of prana in any form and proceeding to the transcendence of the senses and the relinquishment of what is objective by the mind. Whatever be the manner of practice, one must not lose sight of the final goal, which is the egoless state of Self-Realization. However one practices, at last he is brought to this: he must know himself. For that Knowledge, the final Realization, Self-inquiry, the apex of all practice, is the means. How else is one to know the Self except by profoundly, constantly inquiring "Who am I?"

The scriptures have referred to yoga, including the form of ashtanga-yoga, and also to jnana, which can also be viewed in eight aspects. The ashtanga yoga can be found in yoga treatises, while the details of the ashtanga jnana are found expressed in a fifteen-aspect description toward the conclusion of Adi Sankara's *Aparokshanubhuti.* Among scriptural texts, that is, texts pertaining to the Veda-s, both the stages of yoga and jnana are mentioned in various Upanishads, such as yoga in *Amritanada Upanishad* and *Sandilya Upanishad,* while stages of both yoga and jnana are described in *Tejobindu Upanishad.* These two modes of approach are also described in *Ramana Gita.* The Maharshi states that the purpose of such is Self-Realization, and the yoga practices employed are for control of the mind. The control of the mind should lead to a withdrawal from the external objects, or the abandonment of misidentification with the senses and confusion about them regarding reality; that is, one should no longer mistake the senses as a means of determining reality and should abandon the ignorant conception of the world.

For the benefit of the disciple, the Maharshi sets forth these paths, beginning with a description of ashtanga (eight limbed) yoga and a description of jnana in eight limbs, the latter appearing later in this *Self-Inquiry.*

Self-Realization is the fruit of inquiry. Thus declares the all-knowing great rishi. Whoever practices ardently for union with the indivisible Absolute, which is none other than the true Self of all, being blessed with the Maharshi's teachings, which are of such clarity that even crystal and air cannot compare, and with this grace by the power of which all efforts for Realization bear fruit and not the least effort goes in vain, finds Absolute Knowledge and, with the mind absorbed forever herein, abides in infinite Wisdom and Bliss.

Om Sri Ramanarpanamastu
Om May this be an offering to Sri Ramana

27

Disciple: What are the limbs of yoga?

The Maharshi: Yama, niyama, asana, pranayama, pratyahara, dharana, dhyana, and samadhi. Of these—

(1) Yama:—this stands for the cultivation of such principles of good conduct as non-violence (ahimsa), truth (satya), non-stealing (asteya), celibacy (brahmacharya), and non-possession (aparigraha).

Commentary:

Om Namo Bhagavate Sri Ramanaya

The limbs of yoga are named and the traditional techniques are described. Yama involves the abstention from activities that are the crude forms of ignorance. Yama is not only for the purpose of good karma and the elimination of bad karma, but it is for the purpose of eliminating from the mind the causes of that from which one abstains. One must be first free from anger, wrath, or frustration; dishonesty and insincerity, greed and avarice, lust or craving, and possessiveness and attachment in order to attain union (yoga) with the Supreme. One who practices yama should advance to feel that such is no abstention but is natural.

The Maharshi:

(2) Niyama:—this stands for the observance of such rules of good conduct as purity (saucha), contentment (santosha), austerity (tapas), study of the sacred texts (svadhyaya), and devotion to God (Isvarapranidhana).

Commentary:

Niyama is next described. Purity extends from right intention and relates to sattva. What constitutes purity is dealt with extensively and in various manners in many scriptures. Contentment should be the basic attitude of one who is intent upon Realization, who knows that the objects and conditions of the world are unrelated to one's happiness and peace, and who is diving within to experience that happiness and peace. With santosha, one does not make a grievance over what does not please one, but rather one develops greater detachment and relinquishes the tendency of opining with the mind. Tapas is fiery practice, the light of which destroys the darkness of ignorance, the heat of which melts or burns all of delusion's dross. It may also be understood as austerity, the physical act of which by itself is not of much significance, but when based upon nonattachment and fascination with the Bliss of the Self is truly glorious. The study of the sacred texts, be they Veda-s or Agama-s, *Siva Rahasya* or *Mahabharata,* Upanishad-s or Purana-s, teachings of wise sages or legends about the divine, informs the mind of what should be known. Though the Realization of the Self is ineffable, it is a great blessing for aspirants that such texts exist and have been preserved, giving description to the ineffable, conveying Knowledge about the non-conceptual, and inspiring and illuminating the reader. Such scriptural study should be done meditatively with an aim to enter the experience of the Knowledge revealed and to have the inner darshanam of the sages whose utterances are contained therein. Quantity of texts read is utterly insignificant. To experience what is related in the scriptures is what is of utmost importance. Lastly, devotion to God is mentioned. This attenuates the ego and is the support and purpose of the other aspects of niyama. One should realize that God is alone real and devotion to God alone matters; the ego and its concerns are utterly insignificant.

The Maharshi:
(3) Asana:—Of the different postures, eighty-four are the main ones. Of these, again, four, viz., simha, bhadra, padma, and siddha, are said to be excellent. Of these too, it is only siddha that is the most excellent. Thus the yoga-texts declare.

Commentary:
The various asana-s are regarded as having various effects upon one's meditation, especially in a subtle sense, until one abandons misidentification with the body and the introversion of the mind no longer depends on posture, activity, etc. The aim of asana should be to attain a state in which meditation continues undisturbed by bodily posture. Once one has transcended the attachment to the body or to

the sensations of the body, asana is irrelevant. The Self itself has no asana.

The Maharshi:

(4) Pranayama:—According to the measures prescribed in the sacred texts, exhaling the vital air is rechaka, inhaling is puraka and retaining it in the heart is kumbhaka. As regards "measure," some texts say that rechaka and puraka should be equal in measure, and kumbhaka twice that measure, while other texts say that if rechaka is one measure, puraka should be of two measures, and kumbhaka of four. By "measure" what is meant is the time that would be taken for the utterance of the Gayatri mantra once. Thus pranayama consisting of rechaka, puraka, and kumbhaka should be practiced daily according to ability, slowly and gradually. Then, there would arise for the mind a desire to rest in happiness without moving. After this, one should practice pratyahara.

Commentary:

The aim behind pranayama has already been explained. The direct path to Self-Realization has also already been explained. Explained, too, are the reasons to practice and not to practice yoga methods and the invariable necessity for Self-inquiry yielding Self-Knowledge. Thus, in Bhagavan's Tamil rendition of *Devikalottara*, v. 16, it is stated, "Holding of the breath, muttering of a miscellany of mantra-s, practices such as stambhava (stoppage of vital air movements), concentration, all these those desirous of undecaying Liberation do not have to endeavor to cultivate." In the Sanskrit *Sri Devikalottara (Jnanacaravicara Patalah)*, the same verse is, "Holding the breath, miscellany of mantra-s, controlling the vital airs, and concentration of the mind, all such should not be practiced by one who desires undecaying Liberation."

Here details of control of prana through manipulation of the rhythm of the breath are described. Pranayama is also practiced at the time of japa (repetition of a mantra) of Gayatri mantra by those who are initiated into it, and the time of one repetition is here utilized as a unit of measure.

The mantra itself is,

ॐ भूर्भुवः स्वः ।
तत्सवितुर्वरेण्यं
भर्गो देवस्य धीमहि
धियो यो नः प्रचोदयात् ॥

om bhūr-bhuvaḥ svaḥ |
tat-savitur-vareṇyaṁ
bhargo devasya dhīmahi
dhiyo yo naḥ pracodayāt ||

The first line is recited with it, though the remainder alone is properly the Gayatri as it appears in *Ṛg Veda* III, 62:10. The significance of it is Om, the earth, the atmosphere, and the heavens (the meditator should contemplate all of these at once). That Savitur (God as the Light of the sun, associated with the time right before dawn, the vivifier) is the God to be worshipped (or upon which we meditate); may it enlighten (or impel) our minds.

When the desire to find happiness becomes the desire for the mind to rest unmovingly in bliss, one proceeds beyond the domain of prana to pratyahara.

The Maharshi:

(5) Pratyahara:—This is regulating the mind by preventing it from flowing towards external names and forms. The mind, which had been till then distracted, now becomes controlled. The aids in this respect are (1) meditation on the pranava, (2) fixing the attention betwixt the eye-brows, (3) looking at the tip of the nose, and (4) reflection on the nada. The mind that has thus become one-pointed will be fit to stay in one place. After this, dharana should be practised.

Commentary:

If the mind ceases to be fixated on the external forms and ideas about them, it liberates itself from the senses and is no longer distracted by them. Meditation will be firm and steady for one who does not abandon it just because some sensory impression, such as a sound, a sight, a sensation, a taste, or a scent, has occurred. Such a one feels, "There have been countless sensory experiences. None of them endure; none of them are happiness or peace. Why focus upon them when it is the Self that is to be realized?" However, since the aforementioned ripeness for inquiry into the Self is considered as missing for the seeker about whom these series of questions and answers are concerned, other techniques to catch the mind's attention are mentioned. By holding on to them, the mind will not drift along the channels of the old tendencies to fixate on the unreal sense objects.

Pranava refers to meditation on Om. This can be performed as meditation upon the sound Om, or as meditation on Om as continuous, eternal, and pervading the entire universe, or as that which exists as "the higher and lower" as Dattatreya declares in *Avadhuta Gita,* and constituting yet transcending the three states as revealed by *Mandukya Upanishad* with the *Karika* by Sri Gaudapada, "The letter Om is all this... All that is past, present, or future is only Om. That which is beyond the three times is also only Om." 1:1; "Om is Brahman, beyond fear" 1:25. "Om is Brahman. Om is all this." *(Taittiriya Upanishad,* 1:8:1) "Om is indeed all this." *(Chandogya Upanishad* II, 33:3) "Meditate on the Self thus with the help of Om." *(Mundaka Upanishad* 2:6)

Meditation upon the location ascribed to the "third eye," which also has a transcendent, formless, bodiless significance as when depicted on murti-s (icons) of Siva, gazing with fixed attention at the tip of the nose mentioned in *Bhagavad Gita,* and focussing upon nada, subtle sound, are all techniques utilized to enhance this pratyahara. In all cases, the aim is to rise above distraction caused by the mind's agitation over external objects and sensory experiences so that meditation may become more concentrated or one-pointed and free from interruptions.

The Maharshi:

(6) Dharana: This is fixing the mind in a locus that is fit for meditation. The loci that are eminently fit for meditation are the heart and Brahma-randhra (aperture in the crown of the head). One should think that in the middle of

the eight-petalled lotus that is at this place there shines, like a flame, the deity, which is the Self, i.e., Brahman, and fix the mind therein. After this, one should meditate.

Commentary:

Here, dharana, or concentration, is described. Meditation upon Brahman, or the Self, is brought in at this level, but appearing as the deity of the center or cakra utilized for this practice. The visualization of these centers, such as Brahma-randhra and the heart are described variously in the Upanishads, Tantra-s, and elsewhere. After this, one leaves behind all consideration of a body, gross or subtle, along with ways of envisioning the Absolute by superimposing form upon it, and proceeds with a mind ripe for meditation, in a more formless manner. The aim of dharana is to be free of distracting thoughts.

The Maharshi:

(7) Dhyana:—This is meditation, through the "I am He" thought, that one is not different from the nature of the aforesaid flame. Even, thus, if one makes the inquiry "Who am I?", then, as the scripture declares, "The Brahman, which is everywhere, shines in the heart as the Self that is the witness of the intellect," and one would realize that it is the Divine Self that shines in the heart as "I-I." This mode of reflection is the best meditation.

Commentary:

Sri Bhagavan now speaks of meditation, having dispensed with the preliminaries. Two meditations are described. First, that of So'ham, "He am I." The declaration is a statement of identity: That exists only as the Self and not something objective or removed from one's Being; the Self is That and not individualized or separate from That. The potential limitation in the practice of such meditation is that of mere repetition as a mantra, or the mere assertion or repetition within the mind of the thought of "I am He" instead of the experience of the truth of it beyond thought. To experience the Truth of identity, one must know oneself, and for this, the inquiry "Who am I?" is the principal means.

By inquiry one realizes that Brahman, which exists everywhere, shining as infinite Consciousness, is the Self in the heart, the quintessence of Being. It is the Self, shining as "I-I," perpetual, uninterrupted Being. The divine Self is the only Self, and you are That. Inquiry reveals this Truth. By inquiry, one abides as the silent Witness, of the nature of pure Consciousness, free from the mind or intellect, ever free of even the least notion. Inquiry does not make one Brahman or the Supreme Self; it reveals one's identity as that Self, Brahman, and the fact that it alone exists. Therefore, this kind of meditation—inquiry into the Self—is regarded as the best by the wise. In a formless way, it reveals the Formless. It is not an approach of "becoming," but rather it reveals ever-existent, real Being. It does not include any of the dualisms and suppositions one is attempting to transcend. It is of the very essence of wisdom and results in unconditional bliss. Therefore, it is declared to be the best.

In Gambhiram Seshayya's notebook, the Maharshi is quoted as saying: "The scripture says, 'Brahman is everywhere and in the human heart as Witness of the mind.' To inquire 'What is that mind?', that is to say, 'Who am I?,' is the inquiry, started on the basis of the scriptural text. The result of this inquiry is that Brahman is found to be in the heart and is felt as 'I-I.' All this is meditation."

Brahman is infinite Being, which is undifferentiated and nondual. Being such, it is declared to be everywhere. It is all in all at all times and places, and it is, itself, timeless and spaceless, with nothing else whatsoever. As there exists none other, it is one's only Self. As it is nonobjective, it is said to be within the heart, abiding as the quintessence of one's Existence. Being of the nature of Consciousness, it is the witness of the mind. Consciousness plus the appearance, or notion, of a mind is termed "the Witness." When, by Self-inquiry, one knows Consciousness as it is, Consciousness knows itself, and, because Consciousness is nondual, nonobjective, and undifferentiated, the witnessed no longer appears. Nondual Consciousness alone abides.

If the mind be inquired into and known in its true nature, it loses its form. Consciousness plus the supposition of existent thought appears as the mind. The thoughts have no existence independent of Consciousness, though Consciousness exists without thought. What has only dependent existence is mere illusory appearance and has no actual existence at all. The only existence of the mind, therefore, is Consciousness. That Consciousness is the Self, the true nature of "I." The mind is only "I," and there is no other "I" than the Self, for the individual ego or mind does not exist. To know the nature of the mind, inquire, "Who am I?".

For one desiring Self-Realization, such desire cannot be said to derive from the ego, but rather it is an intuition of one's natural state. The scriptures, be they ancient or the present revelations of the Maharshi, manifest as a strong basis and guiding light for the inquiry. That which recognizes their Truth in the heart of the aspirant cannot be the ego, for the ego has neither existence nor capacity to know. It is the continuous, eternal Existence within that comprehends and may be said to awaken to the Knowledge of itself revealed by itself. Thus, meditation is the inquiry into the nature of the meditator.

The Maharshi:

(8) Samadhi:—As a result of the fruition of the aforesaid meditation, the mind gets resolved in the object of meditation without harboring the ideas "I am such and such; I am doing this and this." This subtle state in which even the thought "I-I" disappears is samadhi. If one practices this every day, seeing to it that sleep does not supervene, God will soon confer on one the supreme state of quiescence of mind.

Commentary:

The culmination of yoga is samadhi. It is the result of the meditation described above. If completely absorbed in meditation, having left the illusion of the world, the body, the prana, and thoughts, one also relinquishes the misidentifications of being anything or doing anything—even the notion of "I am meditating; I am That," even the notion of "I" or the faintest idea of a Self behind the "I"—that which remains is samadhi, which is Being absorbed in itself, nonobjective Consciousness. "Every day" should be understood as "regularly" or as "always." "Sleep" refers to deep sleep, in which thought is absent. As a causal state, it contains the potential for dream and the appearance of the waking state. Thus waking and dream are constituted of both the causes and effects of ignorance, which are both veiling and the imaginary projection of multiplicity, while deep sleep retains only a cause with no effect, the veiling of Reality but no imaginary duality. Samadhi is characterized by the absence of both cause and effect, subject and object, veiling and multiplicity. If the inquiry is bright and steady, one will not fade from samadhi into sleep or mistake deep sleep for samadhi. If sleep supervenes and one meditates on oneself as Consciousness, the witness of all three states, transcendent of the presence or absence of anything, one is again in samadhi. By remaining absorbed in the Self, samadhi, the highest quiescence, is realized. It does not come by the ego's efforts but is the supreme state due to grace. When self-effort in the form of Self-inquiry meets with divine grace, the supreme good results. That which exists without an alternative is the natural, innate state of Sahaja Samadhi. In That, Grace and the Self are identical, and such is the only Reality. It is abidance in infinite Wisdom and Bliss.

Whoever, having traversed whatever is necessary for him, comes to be absorbed in the Supreme State in which God, Grace, and the Self are identical and remains free from even the least trace of any notion, with neither ego nor anything else to disturb him, abides in infinite Wisdom and Bliss.

Om Sri Ramanarpanamastu
Om May this be an offering to Sri Ramana

28

Disciple: What is the purport of the teaching that in pratyahara one should meditate on the pranava?

The Maharshi: The purport of prescribing meditation on the pranava is this. The pranava is Omkara consisting of three and a half matras, viz., "a," "u," "m," and ardha-matra. Of these, "a" stands for the waking state, Visva-jiva, and the gross body; "u" stands for the dream-state, Taijasa-jiva, and the subtle body; "m" stands for the sleep-state, Prajna-jiva, and the causal body; the ardha-matra represents the Turiya, which is the self or "I"-nature; and what is beyond that is the state of Turiyatita, or pure Bliss. The fourth state, which is the state of 'I'-nature, was referred to in the section on meditation (dhyana): this has been variously described—as of the nature of amatra which includes the three matra-s, "a," "u," "m," as maunakshara (silence-syllable); as ajapa (as muttering without muttering) and as the Advaita-mantra, which is the essence of all mantras such as panchakshara. In order to get at this true significance, one should meditate on the pranava. This is meditation that is of the nature of devotion consisting in reflection on the truth of the Self. The fruition of this process is samadhi, which yields release, which is the state of unexcellable bliss. The revered Gurus also have said that release is to be gained only by devotion that is of the nature of reflection on the truth of the Self.

Commentary:

Om Namo Bhagavate Sri Ramanaya

"Significance of Om unrivalled—unsurpassed who can comprehend Thee?" These words of Sri Ramana appear in the thirteenth verse of *Akshara Mana Malai,* the *Marital Garland of Letters,* addressed to Sri Arunachala. There ever exists That, the incomprehensible, peerless, secondless Reality, which is indescribable, inconceivable, illimitable, and indivisible. It is called Siva, referred to as Brahman, and realized as the Atman. To indicate it, there is a word. It figures in the Veda-s, an Upanishad expounds upon it, other Upanishads speak of it, and it lends its blessedness before every holy name when a namavali is recited. It heralds the perfect fullness, purnam (Om purnamadah...) and signifies the very source of peace (Om Shantih, etc.). The entire royal court intoned it when Vasishtha was to start a discourse replete with wisdom, and for many a yogi and rishi it has been the last sound murmured, dissolving into eternal silence. It is: Om (Aum).

In response to the disciple's request, the Maharshi reveals the secret of Om in a manner similar to verses 8 through 12 of the *Mandukya Upanishad.* Pranava and Omkara are synonymous with "Om." The Omkara is said to be of three and a half matra-s (matra means a measure or a metrical unit or time of one short vowel); that is, it is composed of the three letters "a," "u," "m," plus ardha-matra (half a short syllable). The "a" represents the waking state, "u" the dream state, and "m" the deep sleep state. The three jiva-s mentioned—Visva, Taijasa, and Prajna—are the experiencers of the three states respectively, and each is endowed with an instrument of experience, gross, subtle, or causal. The triads appear as long as the jiva, which is the definition of being an individual experiencer, and the experiences are regarded as real. When individuality in any form and the object of experience in any form are negated by clear inquiry, the triads no longer appear, and only one Consciousness remains. That one Consciousness, which appeared as the three, but also is beyond the three—all-pervasive and all-transcendent—is Om.

The ardha-matra represents Turiya, the Fourth, which is the nature of the "I," free of, yet still viewed in relation to, the three states. Thus the ardha-matra may be regarded as signifying the disappearance into silence. When the Self is realized as it is, it is perpetually in its own natural state of unmodified Bliss, which admits of no multiplicity whatsoever, and this is known as Turiyatita, "beyond the fourth." In *Siva Purana,* in the second recounting of the episode of the infinite column of the Light of Siva, associated with Arunachala, in the *Rudrasamhita* 8:1-10, Brahma narrates,

Brahma said:
1-2. O most excellent sage, we were eager to have a vision of the Lord. Our haughtiness had been curbed. O sage, we waited there patiently. Siva, the protector of the distressed, remover of the haughtiness of the haughty and the undecaying Lord of everything took mercy on us.

3. There arose the sound "Om, Om" in the prolated accent. It was very clear. The divine sound in the form of a word came out from the most excellent of Gods.

4-5. "What shall be this great sound? Thinking like this, I stood perplexed. Vishnu, who is worthy of respect from all the Gods, who is free from all inimical thoughts, saw, with the delightful heart, the eternal Being's manifestation on the right side of the linga. First, he saw the syllable "A," and he saw the syllable "U" thereafter.

6-10. He saw the syllable "M" in the middle and Nada (the mystical sound) in the form "Om" in the end. He saw the first syllable on the right like the blazing sphere of the sun. O foremost of sages, thereafter he saw the syllable "U" dazzling like fire. In the middle he saw the syllable "M" glittering like the lunar sphere. Above that, what he saw was the supreme Brahman, the greatest refuge. It had the lustre of pure crystal. It was the pure Being beyond the Fourth (Turiya), the unsullied, and free from extraneous harassment. It was free from mutually clashing opposites. It was single (isolated), void, free from exterior and interior, though stationed in the exterior and the interior, devoid of beginning, middle and end, the primordial cause of Bliss, the Truth, the Bliss and the Nectar. *(Siva Purana,* J.L. Shastri, 1970 ed., repr. 1981, Motilal Banarsidass, Varanasi.)

Sri Bhagavan declares the fourth state to be of the "I"-nature and proceeds, because of the questioner's request, to describe it in terms of mantra. Mantra has for its root meaning "instrument of thought." Understood as a sacred verse, phrase, or word, it is "that which saves one who reflects or meditates upon it." Sri Bhagavan, in his divine, unsurpassed wisdom, reveals the inner, highest meaning of pranava and other terms relating to mantra.

The one Reality symbolized by Om is also referred to as amatra (measureless, boundless), which contains within itself the three states represented by the three matra-s of "a," "u," "m." It is all in all. It is maunakshara, the syllable of Silence—the indestructible Silence—which can be neither conceived nor uttered. It is the essence of ajapa (continuous mantra without verbal expression; ajapa specifically refers to "hamsa" mantra or "So'ham"—"He am I"— said to be produced naturally, even by the breath, without effort and with no utterance). It is the Advaita-mantra, the mantra of Nonduality, which is proclaimed to be the essence of all mantra-s such as panchakshara (Namah Sivaya—Salutations to Siva).

Therefore, such is not mantra as may be commonly comprehended, but speaking of it as "mantra," the Maharshi reveals the continuous, silent Knowledge that liberates one from all ignorance. It is the self-effulgent Self, Brahman itself, free of all duality, abiding in its own true nature. Thus, Ribhu declares in the Sanskrit *Ribhu Gita* 6:42-61,

42. . . . This is the best mantra of all. All this is, indeed, the Supreme Brahman. I am Brahman alone.

43. I am Brahman. I am pure. I am always pure, ever. I am without qualities. I am without desires. This is the best mantra of all.

44. I am of the nature of Hari, Brahma, and the others. I am also not any of these differentiations. I am just Brahman alone. I am Kaivalya. I am the unsurpassed.

45. I, myself, shine by myself, by myself alone, and not by anything else. I abide in myself. This is the best mantra of all. I, myself, enjoy myself. I, myself, revel in myself. I, myself, am my own Light. I, myself, revel in myself.

46. I, myself, revel in my own Self. I see only my own Self. I am happy in my own Self. This mantra, thus, is the best. I remain in my own Consciousness. I revel in joy in the realm of my Self. I am seated on the throne of my own Self. This is, thus, the best mantra.

47. Ever seeing the mantra of one's Self, ever exercising (practicing) the Knowledge of one's Self, the mantra "I-am-Brahman-I-am" will destroy all sins relating to one's Self.

48. The mantra "I-am-Brahman-I-am" will destroy the defect of duality. "I-am-Brahman-I-am" will destroy the sorrow of differentiation.

49. The mantra "I-am-Brahman-I-am" will destroy the disease of thought. The mantra "I-am-Brahman-I-am" will destroy the disease of intellect.

50. The mantra "I-am-Brahman-I-am" will destroy the disease of mental agony. The mantra "I-am-Brahman-I-am" will destroy all the worlds.

51. The mantra "I-am-Brahman-I-am" will destroy the defect of desire. The mantra "I-am Brahman-I-am" will destroy the defect of anger.

52. The mantra "I-am-Brahman-I-am" will destroy the defect of conceptualizing. The mantra "I-am-Brahman-I-am" will also destroy sankalpa.

53. The mantra "I-am-Brahman-I-am" will destroy the sorrow pertaining to all this. The mantra "I-am-Brahman-I-am" will burn up the blemish of lack of discrimination.

54. The mantra "I-am-Brahman-I-am" will utterly destroy ignorance. The mantra "I-am-Brahman-I-am" will destroy millions of defects.

55. The mantra "I-am-Brahman-I-am" will do away with all rituals. The mantra "I-am-Brahman-I-am" will destroy mistaken notions of the body.

56. The mantra "I-am-Brahman-I-am" will efface [the distinction of] the seen and the unseen. The mantra "I-am-Brahman-I-am" will reveal the Knowledge of the Self.

57. The mantra "I-am-Brahman-I-am" bestows success in the realm of the Self. The mantra "I-am-Brahman-I-am" will destroy the unreality and such.

58. The mantra "I-am-Brahman-I-am" will destroy all else. The mantra "I-am-Brahman-I-am" will confer indescribable joy.

59. The mantra "I-am-Brahman-I-am" will remove the idea of non-Self. The mantra "I-am-Brahman-I-am" confers the bliss of Knowledge.

60. Completely abondoning all mantras, renouncing the seven million great mantra-s, which can only confer hundreds of millions of births, one should resort to the japa of this one mantra.

61. Immediately, one attains Liberation. There is no doubt of this for me. Thus, the explanation of the mantra has been told, the secret in all the millions of Vedas. Whoever hears this even once becomes Brahman oneself.

62. That mind is fit for the supreme Liberation that is aware that He alone is the One who is the ever-blissful, the source of supreme joy, the permanent, from whom there is nothing apart, from whom have been born all the worlds, who cannot be comprehended by words or mind or the assemblage of senses or the body, who is indivisible, who is the physician for the ills of the world, and who is Isvara.

In the Tamil *Ribhu Gita,* the verses appear thus:

16. Thus have I told you about the easy way
     Of having a purificatory bath in the waters of the
        Supreme Brahman.
     Son! whoever hears this even once and understands it
     Will become Brahman.
     Hear now the mantra of the Supreme Brahman,
     As taught by the Supreme Siva.
     At all times this is the best,
     The essence of all great mantras.

17. I am ever Brahman—Existence.
   I am ever Brahman—Consciousness.
   I am ever Brahman—Bliss.
   I am ever Brahman—the pure.
   I am ever Brahman—the nondual.
   I am ever the undivided Supreme Brahman.
   This egoless I-am-Brahman certitude
   Is, indeed, the mantra superior to all.

18. I am Brahman, which is the cause of all.
   I am Brahman, which is the all complete.
   I am Brahman, which is distinct from all.
   I am Brahman, which has not an atom apart.
   I am Brahman, which is established as "I."
   I am ever the undivided Supreme Brahman.
   This egoless I-am-Brahman certitude
   Is, indeed, the mantra superior to all.

19. I am Brahman without delusion.
   I am Brahman without any change of nature
      (vikara) due to maya (illusion, delusion).
   I am ever Brahman, which is without nescience.
   I am Brahman, which has no transformation due
      to this.
   I am Brahman, which has no duality.
   I am ever the One Supreme Brahman.
   This egoless I-am-Brahman certitude
   Is, indeed, the mantra superior to all.

20. I am ever Brahman, the mass of Existence.
   I am ever Brahman, Existence alone.
   I am ever Brahman, the mass of Consciousness.
   I am ever Brahman, Consciousness alone.
   I am ever Brahman, the mass of Bliss.
   I am ever the subtle Supreme Brahman.
   This egoless I-am-Brahman certitude
   Is, indeed, the mantra superior to all.

21. I am ever the Supreme Brahman, the eternal.
I am ever the Supreme Brahman, the pure.
I am ever the Supreme Brahman, the
    knowledgeable.
I am ever the Supreme Brahman, the liberated.
I am ever the Supreme Brahman, the blemishless.
I am ever the undivided Supreme Brahman.
This egoless I-am-Brahman certitude
Is, indeed, the mantra superior to all.

22. I am ever of the nature of exalted Knowledge.
I am ever of the nature of the Supreme Self.
I am ever of the nature of the Supreme Siva.
I am ever of the nature of the immaculate.
I am ever of the nature that is higher than the
    highest.
I am ever of the nature of the Supreme Brahman.
This egoless I-am-Brahman certitude
Is, indeed, the mantra superior to all.

23. I am ever of the nature that is taintless.
I am ever of the nature that is attributeless.
I am ever of the nature that is veil-less.
I am ever of the nature that is actionless.
I am of the nature that is afflictionless.
I am of the nature of the blemishless Supreme
    Brahman.
This egoless I-am-Brahman certitude
Is, indeed, the mantra superior to all.

24. I am ever of the nature that is attachmentless.
I am ever of the nature that is supremely peaceful.
I am ever of the nature that is unfragmented.
I am ever of the nature that is the Absolute Truth.
I am ever of the nature that is bondageless.
I am ever of the nature of the Supreme Brahman.
This egoless I-am-Brahman certitude
Is, indeed, the mantra superior to all.

25. Though I manifest as all the world, individuals
        (jiva-s), and the Supreme (Para),
    I am of the nature that is totally devoid of all such
        differences.
    I am of the nature of the undivided Essence
    That is to be known by the crest of the Vedas.
    I am ever of the nature of the nondual Supreme
        Brahman,
    Which remains as Existence-Consciousness-Bliss.
    This egoless I-am-Brahman certitude
    Is, indeed, the mantra superior to all.

26. The blemishless Knowledge of the Supreme
    Should be practiced by the daily, constant,
        assiduous repetition
    Of the incomparable mantra,
    I-am-Brahman, for a long time.
    It is the I-am-Brahman mantra alone
    That will destroy all great sins.
    The speckless I-am-Brahman mantra
    Will destroy the distress that dualism develops.

27. The renowned I-am-Brahman mantra alone
    Is that which destroys all false differences.
    The eminent I-am-Brahman mantra alone
    Will destroy all the ills of thought.
    The joyous I-am-Brahman mantra alone
    Will destroy all the ills of the mind.
    The I-am-Brahman mantra alone
    Will destroy various kinds of diseases of the mind.

28. The abiding I-am-Brahman mantra alone
    Will destroy all conceivable sorrow.
    The expansive I-am-Brahman mantra alone
    Will destroy all the desires of the heart.
    The eminent I-am-Brahman mantra alone
    Will destroy all the swollen anger.
    The great I-am-Brahman mantra alone
    Will destroy all concepts (sankalpa).

29. The I-am-Brahman mantra alone, when uttered,
    Will destroy manifold thoughts.
    The expansive I-am-Brahman mantra alone
    Will destroy all the miseries of "I."
    The faultless I-am-Brahman mantra alone
    Will destroy all the miseries of "this."
    The eminent I-am-Brahman mantra alone
    Will destroy all appearances.

30. The pure I-am-Brahman mantra alone
    Will destroy all ignorance.
    The pure I-am-Brahman mantra alone
    Will destroy all lack of discrimination.
    The pure I-am-Brahman mantra alone
    Will destroy all conceit.
    The pure I-am-Brahman mantra alone
    Will destroy the misery of mundane existence.

31. The eminent I-am-Brahman mantra alone
    Will destroy all the defects of the concept of "body."
    The faultless I-am-Brahman mantra alone
    Will destroy all the defects of the concept
        of "senses."
    The joyous I-am-Brahman mantra alone
    Will destroy the defects of the concept of "mind"
        and such.
    The I-am-Brahman mantra alone, when uttered,
    Will, indeed, destroy millions of defects.

32. The uplifting I-am-Brahman mantra alone
    Will destroy all yantra-s (mystic diagrams) and
        tantra-s (rituals).
    The clarifying I-am-Brahman mantra alone
    Will destroy all the manifest and the unmanifest.
    The transforming I-am-Brahman mantra alone
    Will destroy all unreal delusion.
    The revealing I-am-Brahman mantra alone
    Will destroy any kind of duality.

33. The cherished I-am-Brahman mantra alone
Will destroy all the elements.
The revealing I-am-Brahman mantra alone
Will destroy all the series of worlds.
The transforming I-am-Brahman mantra alone
Will efface all feeling of non-Self.
The resounding I-am-Brahman mantra alone
Will remove the world, the individuals (jiva-s) and
the Supreme (Para).

34. The resounding I-am-Brahman mantra alone
Will bring continuous meditation.
The resounding I-am-Brahman mantra alone
Will bring on savikalpa (differentiated) samadhi.
The resounding I-am-Brahman mantra alone
Will bring on the samadhi without vikalpa (false
notion, difference, diversity).
The resounding I-am-Brahman mantra
Invokes immediate Awareness.

35. The peerless I-am-Brahman mantra alone
Procures the pleasure of goodness.
The faultless I-am-Brahman mantra alone
Yields the perception of power.
The I-am-Brahman mantra alone, when uttered,
Brings in the perception of absence of categories.
The faultless I-am-Brahman mantra alone
Brings in the perception of the fourth state.

36. It is ever the I-am-Brahman mantra
That reveals the blemishless Knowledge of the Self.
It is ever the I-am-Brahman mantra
That affords conquest of the blemishless world of
the Self (Atmaloka).
It is ever the I-am-Brahman mantra
That gives the wonderful Bliss of the Self.
It is ever the I-am-Brahman mantra
That gives the undivided Bliss of Liberation.

37. There is no mantra at all
    To surpass the I-am-Brahman mantra,
    As the seven crores of mighty mantras
    Result only in several crores of births
    And do not alter, in the least, the succession of
        births.
    The blemishless I-am-Brahman mantra, greater
        than all,
    Should, hence, be resorted to,
    And all other mantras should be discarded.

38. Casting aside all kinds of mantras,
    All seekers after Liberation should,
    Firmly, assiduously, and uninterruptedly
    Practice the I-am-Brahman mantra, ever.
    By such changeless practice,
    Knowledge (Jnana) and Liberation (Moksha), all—
        will be attained in a moment.
    Touching the feet of the Supreme Siva who presides
        over all,
    I say this as the Truth. There is no doubt of this.

39. Nidagha! I have explained to you
    This meaning, highly secret in all the Vedas,
    Vedanta, all epics, all scriptures,
    As expounded to me,
    For the benefit of all,
    By the Lord (Isvara), the Awareness of Truth, the
        mass of Bliss.
    Whoever hears and understands this
    Will become the perfectly full Supreme Brahman.

40. All that is seen in imagination is ever illusory.
    The blemishless Supreme Siva is the only Truth.
    The Knowledge that "I am That,"
    Beyond the reach of the mind, of speech, and of any
        of the infirm senses—
    The great mass of Knowledge-Bliss—
    Is the only proper means of Liberation.

This is certain.
Thus did Ribhu teach the fearless mantra for the bath.

41. It is the perfectly full form of our Lord in a state of
    joyous dance that speaks of the sublime Truth—
    I am the immutable, taintless, attributeless,
      eternal,
    Partless, blemishless, differenceless, perfectly full
      Existence-Consciousness-Bliss, Brahman—
    And that gives the sublime bath and the pure
      mantra I-am-Brahman.

The one Reality is the true significance of these details
of the esoteric, nondual meaning of mantra. Since the most
ancient of times, meditation on pranava has been recommended by the wise seers of the Supreme. Sri Bhagavan says
one should meditate on pranava in such a way that it is the
supreme devotion of meditation on the Truth of the Self. Sri
Adi Sankara declares in *Vivekacudamani*, verse 32,

मोक्षकारणसामग्र्यां भक्तिरेव गरीयसी ।
स्वस्वरूपानुसन्धानं भक्तिरित्यभिधीयते ॥

mokṣakāraṇasāmagryāṁ bhaktireva garīyasī |
svasvarūpānusandhānaṁ bhaktirityabhidhīyate ||

and in verse 33,

स्वात्मतत्त्वानुसन्धानं भक्तिरित्यपरे जगुः ॥

svātmatattvānusandhānaṁ bhaktirityapare jaguḥ ||

which may be translated as "Among the means for Liberation (moksha), bhakti (devotion) is, indeed, most important (dearest, valuable). Inquiry into one's own true nature
is said to be bhakti. Others sang that the inquiry into the
Truth of one's own Self (Atman) is devotion (bhakti)." This
is parabhakti (supreme bhakti) and jnana (Knowledge) as
one, the result of which is samadhi (intense absorption). If
samadhi is without form, beginning or end, it is release, or
Liberation, which is unalloyed, highest Bliss, beyond which
there is nothing else.

Who are the revered gurus? They are the ones who abide as the Self, as Brahman itself. The revered gurus are they who are liberated from all, who are the knowers of the Truth, and who stand identified solely as That. They are full of wisdom and grace. Their compassion is boundless, their silence fathomless. They, being illumination itself, destroy all darkness. They bring one from darkness to Light, from the unreal to the Real, and from death to immortality. It is not possible to give an adequate description of such a guru. Such a guru is Bhagavan Sri Ramana Maharshi, and so fortunate are his disciples and devotees.

"Devotion that is of the nature of reflection on the Truth of the Self" is declared by the revered guru to be the only means of attaining Liberation. Whatever be the approach, if a sadhana (spiritual practice) is to culminate in Self-Realization, it must, at its finality, become meditation upon the Self. In inquiry, one meditates directly on the Self, relinquishing all that is not the Self and hence unreal. In nondual devotion, all notions of a separate individuality are surrendered. If the devotee meditates on the Supreme as other, then three are being worshipped: The Supreme, the individual (jiva), and the separation. If one's devotion is singular, the jiva and the belief in separation are abandoned, and Liberation is the fruit thereof.

Whoever meditates with single-pointed, unswerving devotion and whoever inquires into the nature of the Self attains the natural state of samadhi, being released from all the illusion of bondage, and, abiding beyond the three experiencers and the three states as That which is all in all at all times, transcendent and immanent, symbolized by Om, dwells forever in infinite Wisdom and Bliss.

Om Sri Ramanarpanamastu
Om May this be an offering to Sri Ramana

29

Disciple: What is the purport of the teaching that one should meditate through the "I am He" thought on the truth that one is not different from the self-luminous Reality that shines like a flame?

The Maharshi: (A) The purport of teaching that one should cultivate the idea that one is not different from the self-luminous Reality is this: Scripture defines meditation in these words, "In the middle of the eight-petalled heart-lotus that is of the nature of all, and which is referred to as Kailasa, Vaikuntha, and Parama-pada, there is the Reality, which is of the size of the thumb, which is dazzling like lightning, and which shines like a flame. By meditating on it, a person gains immortality." From this we should know that by such meditation one avoids the defects of (1) the thought of difference, of the form "I am different, and that is different," (2) the meditation on what is limited, (3) the idea that the Real is limited, and (4) that it is confined to one place.

Commentary:

Om Namo Bhagavate Sri Ramanaya

The Maharshi reveals the most direct form of meditation: meditation on the Self. In this meditation, Being reposes in itself, self-effulgent Consciousness shines its own light in upon itself, Bliss revels in itself. Dualism is effaced and nothing appears as intermediate between oneself and the Self.

To meet the needs of various aspirants, numerous forms of meditation have been devised by wise gurus over the years. One who follows the direct path of pure Advaita Vedanta, the very same revealed by the Maharshi, can perceive the original intent and efficaciousness of these meditations, extracting the pith from the sheath of form. The original intent is invariably to bring about the Realization of the non-difference of the self-luminous Reality and oneself.

The scriptural reference has correspondence, in whole or part, to *Chandogya Upanishad* 8:1:1-3, *Mahanarayana Upanishad* 10:23, *Dhyanabindu Upanishad* 9, *Maha Upanishad* 1:12-4, and *Atmabodha Upanishad* 1:2-4. These refer, in both visualized and absolute terms, to the heart lotus, the city of Brahman, the analogies of luminosity, the three-and-a-half matra-s of Aum, and similar themes of this portion of *Self-Inquiry*. On the one hand, a visualization of the heart lotus is described; on the other, in the same breath, this heart is said to be of the nature of all. The nature of all is necessarily formless, for form implies limit in space and time and differentiation; all forms have boundaries, are transitory, and must be based upon differentiation in order to be perceived or conceived. That which is the nature of all is infinite, eternal, and forever undifferentiated. There can be no separate knower and known in it. It is the infinite space of vast, formless Consciousness. This is the abode of Siva, Kailasa, and the abode of Vishnu, Vaikuntha. Do you wish to have the darshan of Siva or of Vishnu? You must go to their abode. That abode is omnipresent, yet beyond the concept of location, being formless. So how is one to pilgrimage to there? The direction is within. Within is the Self. To reach the Self, one must know oneself. As there is actually no distance between oneself and one's Self, for there are not two selves, the "journey" of Self-Knowledge simply eliminates the ignorant belief in differentiation. The same is true of Paramapada, which may be taken to mean the abode of the Lord but, upon inquiry means the State of the Supreme, which is the true state of the Self. The further imagery of the scriptural text serves to allude to the subtlety, intensity, and steadiness of the Reality, of the nature of pure, self-luminous Consciousness.

"By meditating on it, a person gains immortality." One becomes that upon which one meditates. In inquiry, one becomes what one already truly is. To be as you are is the essence. The Self is unborn and deathless. One who meditates on the Self, the Reality, realizes his unborn, undying, bodiless nature, and, with the dispelling of the fetters of illusion, attains immortality.

The intent of nondual meditation is to enable one to be free of four defects. The first defect is the thought of difference, of the form "I am different, and that is different." This notion manifests as the belief that the meditator and the goal, or object, of meditation are different and as the idea that the "I" is one thing, an experiencer, and "this" is another, an object of experience. The first belief is eliminated by meditating upon the Reality being in the heart, at the very center of oneself, and by the phrase of instruction: "immortality," for nothing will change its nature. Immortality must be intrinsic to the Self. What is mortal will not become immortal. What begins will not become endless. But the beginningless is already endless, and Knowledge reveals it. If the Reality were other than oneself, immortality would not be possible, but such a view is contrary to the word of the scriptures, the guru, and the innate desire to not cease to exist, which is an intuition of our true nature.

The second false belief, or idea, of this defect is negated by "of the nature of all." Being the nature of all, Brahman is the "I," the "this," and the relation between them. Brahman is devoid of experiencer and object of experience. When these are imagined, still they are only Brahman. Even illusion and duality are Brahman. There is only Brahman, ever.

The second defect is meditation on what is limited. That which is limited cannot yield Liberation from all bondage. That which is limited cannot reveal unqualified Being and unconditional Bliss. Limitation pertains to form and is confined to the domain of thought. The Absolute transcends thought and all limits. To realize the Absolute, one's meditation must be on that which is without limits and free from thought. That is the Self. Meditation on what is limited is invariably based upon, or incorporates, suppositions of one's identity as a limited being. Since one becomes that upon which one meditates, one will proceed from one limitation to another. Meditation upon the Self, in the form of inquiry, incorporates no such assumptions and enables one to realize the Absolute Self. The scriptural passages "of the nature of all," "Paramapada," etc., and "a person gains immortality" negate meditation on what is limited.

The third defect is the idea that the Real is limited. Immortality can come only from that which is eternal. What is eternal is also infinite, as it is the experience of all that no finite form is imperishable. What is infinite and eternal is formless, as no form is without limits in space and time. What is formless cannot be limited in any manner, as limits and forms are synonymous. Duality is needed for limitation in order to conceive of the limit and the limited. The undifferentiated, homogeneous, formless Brahman cannot be dual, as the nature of two can arise only after the conception of "I" and form. The formless, nondual, infinite, eternal Brahman is always beyond limitation, for it is as it is, and there is never anything other to limit or to modify it. Moreover, whatever forms appear anywhere at any time are all only That, Brahman, and nothing else. He who contemplates the form does not see Brahman; he who meditates on Brahman as the Self sees no form, but only the undifferentiated Existence, and knows all to be That.

When one meditates on the Reality as if it were separate from the identity of the meditator, this is a superimposition of limitation upon the Reality, because such includes the idea, "Reality extends thus far and no farther, for it is not where I am." In that case, dualism is present as a belief in two existences, or realities, that of "the Reality" and that of "oneself." In such a case, there is merely a notion about Reality and about oneself and not true Knowledge of the Reality of the Self. The defect is negated by the scriptural passages "middle" and "nature of all" and "immortality."

The fourth defect is the notion that it, the Reality, is confined to one place. This defect arises for an aspirant primarily because of the misidentification with the body. It may manifest as a conception that God is in a realm apart from one's own existence, the conceptual assignment of the Self to a particular subtle center, such as a cakra, nadi, etc., the belief that experience of the Self can be had only when the body is in a particular place, such as a temple, tirtha, etc., or in a particular condition, such as active or inactive. If the ignorant "I-am-the-body notion" is destroyed, neither God nor oneself is viewed in bodily terms, and separation vanishes. If body-misidentification is destroyed, there is no false notion of the Self having location in reference to a body, gross or subtle. If the "I-am-the-body" delusion is destroyed, here and there, now and then, and active and inactive are all felt to be the same, and one is continuously meditating in the temple of the endless space of Consciousness. The scriptural passages of "the nature of all" and "Kailasa, Vaikuntha, and Parama-pada" are intended to negate any defect of the notion of confinement to a location, be that notion due to extant delusion or misinterpretation of the images presented in that same portion of the scripture.

Whoever understands Sri Bhagavan's elucidation of the meaning of the ancient scriptures will be endowed with meditation free from all defects, and, endowed with the ability to clearly discern the true purport of the scriptures, will find immortality dwelling in infinite Wisdom and Bliss.

Om Sri Ramanarpanamastu
Om May this be an offering to Sri Ramana

29 *(continued)*

The Maharshi: (B) The purport of the teaching that one should meditate on the "I am He" thought is this: sah aham: so'ham; sah the supreme Self, aham the Self that is manifest as "I." The jiva, which is the Siva-linga, resides in the heart-lotus, which is its seat situated in the body, which is the city of Brahman; the mind, which is of the nature of egoity, goes outward identifying itself with the body, etc. Now, the mind should be resolved in the heart, i.e., the I-sense that is placed in the body, etc., should be got rid of; when thus one enquires "Who am I?", remaining undisturbed, in that state, the Self-nature becomes manifest in a subtle manner as "I-I;" that Self-nature is all and yet none and is manifest as the supreme Self everywhere without the distinction of inner and outer; that shines like a flame, as was stated above, signifying the truth "I am Brahman." If, without meditating on that as being identical with oneself, one imagines it to be different, ignorance will not leave. Hence, the identity-meditation is prescribed.

Commentary:

Om Namo Bhagavate Sri Ramanaya

The aphorisms of wise sages preserved for ages were originally spontaneous utterances expressing their own experience in the course of instructing disciples. They must be received by the seeker of Truth in the same spirit. He must dive deep into their meaning to realize the actual, direct experience expressed. "He am I" (So'ham) is one such expression. It is indicative of meditation on identity, similar to the Mahavakya-s (great sayings) Tat Tvam Asi (That you are), Prajnanam Brahma (Consciousness, or Supreme Knowledge, is Brahman), Ayam Atma Brahma (this Self is Brahman), and Aham Brahmasmi (I am Brahman). The identity realized by Self-inquiry is expressed in these and similar aphorisms. Sri Bhagavan, the all-knowing sage, overflowing with Grace and compassion, and in response to the disciple's need, presents this explanation of this identity-meditation for the spiritual benefit and Liberation of all who receive it.

So'ham declares the identity of Siva and the Self. Siva is the Self and is not otherwise. The Self is Siva and is not otherwise. Sri Adi Sankara states in *Vivekacudamani* v. 270,

ज्ञात्वा स्वं प्रत्यगात्मानं बुद्धितद्वृत्तिसाक्षिणम् ।
सोऽहमित्येव सद्वृत्त्याऽनात्मन्यात्ममतिं जहि ॥

jñātvā svaṁ pratyagātmānaṁ buddhitadvṛttisākṣiṇam|
so'hamityeva sadvṛttyā'nātmanyātmamatiṁ jahi ||

which may be translated as, "Having known your own innermost Self, the witness of the intellect and its modes, by the true mode (true state, good method) of "He I am," indeed, abandon (slay) the idea of the Self in the non-Self." The Maharshi says the phrase of So'ham may be understood to mean sah, the Supreme Self, is aham, I am, or the Self that is manifest as I. The Siva-linga is the manifest sign of the undivided Absolute Reality, Siva. Siva is the supreme Self, unalloyed Existence. Jiva, the individual, is the Siva-linga in the heart, that is, the sign of that Existence within you. The Truth is declared: the jiva is, in reality, Siva. If the individual is sought with inquiry, its individuality vanishes, and the Self alone remains.

The Siva-linga of the jiva is said to reside in the heart-lotus; it is said to be situated in the body, which is to be regarded as the city of Brahman. Existence, which is Siva, is within one's own heart and not apart from oneself. When conceived as being a jiva, the latter appears to have its dwelling in the body. Siva, the Self, is not other than Brahman. Brahman is the formless, all-pervading presence and the indweller of every heart. The whole universe, the body, or the heart may be regarded as the abode of Brahman, the place where Brahman has its life (jiva). Sri Adi Sankara says (*Vivekacudamani* v. 340),

सर्वात्मना बन्धविमुक्तिहेतुः सर्वात्मभावान्न
परोऽस्ति कश्चित् ।
दृश्याग्रहे सत्युपपद्यतेऽसौ सर्वात्मभावोऽस्य
सदात्मनिष्ठया ॥

sarvātmanā bandhavimuktihetuḥ sarvātmabhāvānna
paro'sti kaścit |
dṛśyāgrahe satyupapadyate'sau sarvātmabhāvo'sya
sadātmaniṣṭhayā ||

which may be translated as, "By the Self of all; than the 'All is the Self' conviction, there is nothing better for the means (cause) of complete Liberation from bondage. By insistent negation of the perceived, by abidance always as the Self (as the eternal Self), that 'All is the Self' conviction is reached."

The mind is only the ego in different guises. The mind starts from the ego, depends on the ego, is caused by the ego, and is contained within the ego. When it conjures illusions within itself, imagining these illusions to be real, and regards them as if external to itself, this is called an outward-going mind. The cornerstone of delusion, the sign of the outward mind, the form without which the ego cannot long survive, is the misidentification with the body.

For Self-Realization, one must go back the way one came. The Maharshi's instruction is to resolve the mind into the Heart. The "I"-sense attributed to the body, or which appears as embodied, should be eliminated. The notions of "I-am-the-body" and "I-am-in-the-body" are to be abandoned by the power of inquiry that reveals the bodiless nature of Being. If by inquiry one resolves the mind in the Heart, by realizing one's nature to be free from all notions, the ego and all its consequent delusions are destroyed.

The inquiry to be made so that the Self is realized is summed up in the question "Who am I?" Question earnestly, with utmost intensity, "Who am I?" and the cherished wisdom and bliss will be realized; and what you realize, you are. By inquiring, "Who am I?" liberate yourself from all misidentification—all ignorance—and remain undisturbed. The Self is immutable peace itself. Disturbance is misidentification, the cause of all unhappiness and bondage. If you remain undisturbed, free of misidentification, the nature of the Self is known clearly. It is revealed within as continuous, egoless Being, "I-I."

Being is all. Yet Being is not any thing at all. Nor is there truly any such thing as "all." Being alone is. It is the Supreme Self, the omnipresent, homogeneous Existence. Devoid of inner and outer, it is neither a subject nor an object. Bodiless and worldless, it has no outer. Without a mind and "I"-less, it has no inner. It shines, self-existent, the "flame" of the Upanishadic passage. This Realization of the Self is the Realization of Brahman. It is the Truth: I am Brahman. Knowing and Being the Truth are one and the same.

Ignorance manifests as differentiation. Such is the imagination of what has never come to be. Knowledge is of the undifferentiated. It is the Realization, or direct, continuous, effortless experience of that which ever is. If meditation is to bring about Realization, it must be of a nondual nature; if meditation is based on the erroneous premise of That as being different from oneself, when will Realization, of the nature of non-differentiation, ever dawn? Repeating ignorance in meditation will not make it go away. Just as adding more mud to already muddy water will not make it clearer, so dualistic meditation will not dissolve ignorant dualism.

The Maharshi shows the clear path. Let your meditation be that of identity. Before assuming difference to be the case, first inquire, "Who am I?" and know who you are, what is Real. Whoever inquires in this manner destroys all ignorance, makes it impossible for new ignorance to form, and, endowed with the unceasing meditation of identity, is set free of all misidentification so as to realize the Supreme Self, which is Brahman and which is Siva, and thus abides in infinite Wisdom and Bliss.

29 *(continued)*

The Maharshi: If one meditates for a long time, without disturbance, on the Self ceaselessly with the "I am He" thought, which is the technique of reflection on the Self, the darkness of ignorance, which is in the heart, and all the impediments, which are but the effects of ignorance, will be removed, and the plenary wisdom will be gained.

Thus, realizing the Reality in the heart-cave, which is in the city (of Brahman), viz. the body, is the same as realizing the all-perfect God.

In the city with nine gates, which is the body, the wise one resides at ease.

The body is the temple; the jiva is God (Siva). If one worships Him with the "I am He" thought, one will gain release.

The body that consists of the five sheaths is the cave; the Supreme that resides there is the Lord of the cave. Thus the scriptures declare.

Since the Self is the reality of all the gods, the meditation on the Self, which is oneself, is the greatest of all meditations. All other meditations are included in this. It is for gaining this that the other meditations are prescribed. So, if this is gained, the others are not necessary. Knowing one's Self is knowing God. Without knowing one's Self that meditates, imagining that there is a deity that is different and meditating on it is compared by the great ones to the act of measuring with one's foot one's own shadow and to the search for a trivial conch after throwing away a priceless gem that is already in one's possession.

Commentary:

Om Namo Bhagavate Sri Ramanaya

In the abundance of his grace, Sri Bhagavan continues to bestow the essential spiritual instruction, consuming all doubts and answering all questions in the process. Such a gracious guru leaves no trace of even the possibility of delusion. He is Brahman, itself, revealing itself. He is Siva Himself, destroying all the unreal and remaining Himself as real Being. He is Dakshinamurti, conveying the whole Truth in transcendent Silence. He is Nataraja, whose blissful dance destroys the demon of forgetfulness and, granting grace and illumination, reveals the infinite. He is the one who is the identity of all sages. He lives as their wisdom and peace and shines as their bliss. He is the Self, which dwells in the hearts of all, the beginning, middle and end of all beings. He is the one to be worshipped, and he is beyond all worship. He is the one upon which to meditate, and he is that in which meditator and object of meditation are absent. He is the liberator of the fettered, the copious spring of ever-fresh direct experience for those who thirst for Truth, the awakener of those who are dreaming, the revealer of Truth for those blinded by delusion, the beloved and savior of the devotee, the mahayogi, the timeless rishi, and the perfect jnani.

The Maharshi tells the disciple to meditate, without the disturbance of misidentification and attachment, ceaselessly on the Self. Why ceaselessly? When the meditation of identity is ceaseless, it reveals itself to be the continuous, natural, innate state of Being. When meditating, if one feels the mind's urge to concoct a concept or one thinks, "that is long enough for meditation; now I must return to my usual (deluded) state of mind," or if in the midst of intense, focused meditation, it seems as if one's effort is about to come to an end or the urge for the mind to become inadvertent and to commence illusion occurs, one should apply oneself unreservedly and maintain the meditation, destroying all time barriers. This is meditation "for a long time." The implication is also one of diligence, perseverance, and continuity in spiritual practice. Meditation should be maintained for as long as one wishes to be blissful and free. If one says, "I desire to be blissful always and ever free," his meditation should be perpetual. The meditation must always be that of identity as previously described by Sri Ramana.

Ignorance is like darkness. Self-Knowledge is like the sun. Inquiry is the dawn. By it, all impediments, the obstacles to happiness and peace, are removed. All obstacles are but ignorance. There are no obstacles from external sources, and there are no obstacles inherent in the Self. The obstacles, and any limitation or bondage, are all composed entirely of ignorance. Self-Knowledge destroys ignorance, like the sun the darkness, and the limitless, perfectly full state of true Wisdom remains. This is the supreme attainment, the attainment of which leaves nothing more to be attained, the bliss of which leaves no other happiness to be desired.

Attaining Self-Realization, realizing the Reality of the Self to be one's only identity, the bodily form is felt to be inconsequential. Abiding as the all-perfect God, the wise one is free of the body, referred to as the city of nine gates in *Bhagavad Gita* 5:13, and of what pertains to the body. The *Gita* verse, quoted by the Maharshi according to B. V. Narasimha Swami, reads,

सर्वकर्माणि मनसा संन्यस्यास्ते सुखं वशी ।
नवद्वारे पुरे देही नैव कुर्वन्न कारयन् ॥

sarvakarmāṇi manasā sannyasyāste sukhaṁ vaśī |
navadvāre pure dehī naiva kurvanna kārayan ||

"Renouncing all actions, by the mind, self-controlled, the embodied one rests happily in the city of nine gates, neither acting nor causing to act." Thus, regardless of whether or not the body acts, the wise one, no longer under the influence of ignorance and thus no longer believing that the senses determine his identity or reality, knowing that he never does anything, abides in the happy transcendence of both the body and the mind. He is at ease, knowing he is not in the body when alive and not exiting it when the body is dying. Disidentified from the temple of the body, he is identified with the indwelling God, with individuality effaced. He has inquired into the nature of the jiva and has found Siva alone is. If one worships Him—Siva—with the spirit of identity and the utter effacement of the ego, one gains release, that is, Liberation from all the imagined bondage.

देहो देवालयः प्रोक्तः स जीवः केवलः शिवः ।
त्यजेदज्ञाननिर्माल्यं सोऽहंभावेन पूजयेत् ॥
अभेददर्शनं ज्ञानं

deho devālayaḥ proktaḥ sa jīvaḥ kevalaḥ śivaḥ |
tyajedajñānanirmālyaṁ so'hambhāvena pūjayet | |
abhedadarśanaṁ jñānaṁ

This may be translated as, "The body is said to be a temple of God. The jiva is Siva alone. Cast off (abandon) the blemish of ignorance; worship with the conviction 'He I am.' The vision (perception) of non-difference is Knowledge." Thus declares the *Skandopanishad* verse 10 and the first portion of verse 11. Verse 6 states,

जीवः शिवः शिवो जीवः स जीवः केवलः शिवः ।

jīvaḥ śivaḥ śivo jīvaḥ sa jīvaḥ kevalaḥ śivaḥ |

This may be translated as, "The jiva is Siva. Siva is the jiva. That jiva is Siva alone." The central focus of the entire Upanishad, which appears among the Samanya Vedanta Upanishads, is concerned with the identity of the jiva with Siva. The same Truth of identity is declared innumerable times in *Ribhu Gita* and in several works by Adi Sankara. The same eternal Truth is revealed here by the Maharshi in almost identical words to those that appear in *Skandopanishad*. The Truth of the Self is immutable. Thus, the wisdom of Self-Knowledge remains unchanging age after age, just as it remained all through the years of Sri Bhagavan's gracious revelation of it. The emphasis is not so much upon the temple of the body, but upon whose temple it is. Appearing as if within the form of the body, and as if individualized, is the formless, location-less, space-like Siva, the Absolute Self. Identity as only this Self is the highest devotion and the supreme Knowledge. There is no existence of the individual being except undivided Being. The aim of both devotion and jnana is the abandonment of the ego-notion. That yields Liberation. That is abidance as the Self, which alone is.

The body is said to be of the five sheaths. That is, any form attributed to the Self is merely of the five sheaths: the physical body, the sheath of prana, the sheath of the mind, the sheath of the intellect, and the bliss sheath. Within, at the center of the sheaths, the Lord within the cave abides.

Discriminating keenly between the sheaths and Being-Consciousness, one should merge one's identity with that Lord of the cave.

The scriptures speak of several gods and meditations upon them. The Self is the sole Reality of all the gods. One who meditates on the Self as himself obtains the benefit of all meditations and the blessings of all the gods. He, himself, abides as That which is all of them. All meditations are ultimately intended to secure this state for the meditator. If one whole-heartedly meditates in this pure Advaita manner to know the Self, one has the benefits of all meditations, and the other meditations are not necessary.

Imagining a deity in order to meditate upon it will not cause one to awaken to Reality. Without knowing the nature of the meditator, which is the Self, conceiving of deities in the name of meditation is merely an exercise of imagination. How can one's shadow be measured by one's own foot? The movement of the foot also moves the shadow. No such measurement could be possible. Similarly, it is impossible to know God without knowing oneself. One who knows himself is like a sun ever risen, casting no shadow and of immeasurable light.

This invaluable teaching is the wish-fulfilling, priceless gem. It is already ours. The Self it reveals is already within us. To search for something else is only delusion. Why neglect the treasure of the Self to pursue trivial, objective imaginings? Why look for some other teaching when immediately present there shines the ultimate Truth? Thus, in Gambhiram Seshayya's notebook, the Maharshi is said to have written, "Vasishtha points out that those who see gods outside, when they have the Self in their own hearts, are like persons who cast away the precious gem, kaustubha, and set out in quest of inferior stones." Let us not overlook that which is most immediate. Let us not disregard the wise advice of the sages. Let us not undervalue the invaluable Truth, which is the treasure of bliss and which alone endures for eternity. He who, discarding the worthless, transient unreality, seeks only the Supreme Self, knowing that in That alone lies happiness and peace, finds the Eternal Siva, Sadasiva, and remains content, for what he knows he is.

Whoever holds this precious teaching dear, ceaselessly meditating upon it in a state of identity, does not overlook the Self but realizes it to be the nondual Reality, verily God, abides free of the sheaths, and truly at ease, liberated even here and now—and forever—ceaselessly experiences infinite Wisdom and Peace.

Om Sri Ramanarpanamastu
Om May this be an offering to Sri Ramana

30

Disciple: Even though the heart and the Brahmarandhra alone are the loci fit for meditation, could one meditate, if necessary, on the six mystic centers (adharas)?

The Maharshi: The six mystic centres, etc., which are said to be loci of meditation, are but products of imagination. All these are meant for beginners in yoga. With reference to meditation on the six centres, the Siva-yogins say, "God, who is of the nature of the non-dual, plenary, Consciousness-Self, manifests, sustains, and resolves us all. It is a great sin to spoil that Reality by superimposing on it various names and forms such as Ganapati, Brahma, Vishnu, Rudra, Mahesvara, and Sadasiva," and the Vedantins declare, "All those are but imaginations of the mind." Therefore, if one knows one's Self, which is of the nature of Consciousness that knows everything, one knows everything. The great ones have also said: "When that One is known as it is in Itself, all that has not been known becomes known." If we who are endowed with various thoughts meditate on God that is the Self, we would get rid of the plurality of thoughts by that one thought; and then even that one thought would vanish. This is what is meant by saying that knowing one's Self is knowing God. This knowledge is release.

Commentary:
Om Namo Bhagavate Sri Ramanaya

The all-importance of Self-inquiry has already been declared by Sri Bhagavan. The negation of location for the real Self has already been enunciated by the Maharshi. Nevertheless, the disciple asks about the mystic centers—adharas (locations) or cakra-s— as objects of meditation.

The Maharshi frankly declares all such objects of meditation to be merely products of imagination. His negation of the subtle as imagination presupposes a comprehension that all that is gross is also merely imagination. Sri Bhagavan cites both the Siva-yogins and the Vedantins, in the spirit of Tayumanavar and his *Vedanta-Siddhanta-Samarasa*. The multiplicity of centers and gods—gods presiding over those centers—are all only imaginary, and belief in such imagination only spoils one's experience of Reality. By spoiling is meant the mingling, in imagination, of notions of difference with the Absolute Reality, which is undifferentiated. The negation, as unreal, of all name and form, of the gods in general, and those specifically mentioned here occurs in numerous passages of the *Ribhu Gita,* and the mention here of both Siva-yogins and Vedantins would lend itself to a direct correlation of the *Ribhu Gita* and what is taught here by the Maharshi, as do numerous other passages of *Self-Inquiry* and *Ribhu Gita.*

All such experiences, whether known to be imaginary or thought to be real, appear in and are known by Consciousness alone. This is the case with everything. There is no existence to anything other than Consciousness. If you know Consciousness as it is, you, indeed, know all, for it is possible to know Consciousness only if one's identity is Consciousness. The unknown, that is, inconceivable, knower of all that is known is Consciousness, and that alone is the Self. The mystery of Existence becomes self-evident and Reality is known as it is when one knows Consciousness. Again and again and yet again, the same consistent teaching is bestowed by Sri Bhagavan. It is the same instruction given by every true jnani: Know the Self, which is one's own Self.

The meditation of identity, or Self-inquiry, "Who am I?" may commence with a thought of God and the Self as one. With this thought present, all other notions are dispelled. The significance of that thought, though, transcends all ideas, including that one, and he who meditates upon the meaning finds that all notions vanish, leaving non-conceptual Knowledge alone. This Knowledge, in which God and the Self are the same, is release from all bonds—Liberation.

Here, just as in Sri Bhagavan's *Upadesa Sarah (Saram),* verse 25, and in *Saddarshanam,* verses 21 through 23, the Maharshi reveals the identity of the Self and God. He shows that just as it is erroneous to conceive of the Self as other than God, who is the supreme Consciousness, so it is also erroneous to conceive of God as other than the Self, who is eternally transcendent of all that is objective and the inherent limitations of the objective. According to B. V. Narasimha Swami, Gambhiram Seshayya's original notebook also included this, attributed to the Maharshi, "In fact, when we worship images, we are really worshipping ourselves in the images." He who sees the Self is himself the Self, and thus God sees God with God's own eye.

The truth that, upon Knowledge of the Self, there is nothing else to be known and everything else to be known is known, is found in the Upanishads and in several passages of various sacred works composed by Adi Sankara. Who else is there to know or not know anything, as the Self is utterly nondual? As the Self is unborn, infinite, homogenous, undivided, and invariable, who could there be to know what? Moreover, the quintessence of wisdom is Self-Knowledge, which is the Knowledge of the one Reality. This is revealed with utmost clarity by Sri Bhagavan. Absorbing the nectar of immortality of his gracious Wisdom by being absorbed in it, which is he, himself, what else could one desire to know? It is absolute, and the Realization of that Self is the Knowledge, knowing which there is nothing else to be known and is the Bliss, experiencing which leaves no other happiness to be desired.

Whoever meditates upon the Truth, the nondual unity of God and the Self, realized by the great sages of Vedanta and the Siva-yogi-s, realizes the unreality of all that is imagined, and, dwelling beyond dualism, abiding identified as infinite Consciousness, is himself the infinite Wisdom and Bliss.

Om Sri Ramanarpanamastu
Om May this be an offering to Sri Ramana

31

Disciple: How is one to think of the Self?

The Maharshi: The Self is self-luminous, without darkness and light, and is the Reality, which is self-manifest. Therefore, one should not think of it as this or as that. The very thought of thinking will end in bondage. The purport of meditation on the Self is to make the mind take the form of the Self. In the middle of the heart-cave the pure Brahman is directly manifest as the Self in the form "I-I." Can there be greater ignorance than to think of it in manifold ways, without knowing it as aforementioned?

Commentary:

Om Namo Bhagavate Sri Ramanaya

Reality, of the nature of Being-Consciousness-Bliss, transcends all thought. Knowledge of Reality is not composed of a set of thoughts. Advaita Vedanta is not a doctrine of ideas, however lofty. The final Knowledge of Nonduality—Advaita Vedanta—is the direct experience of Reality by Reality itself. The Self is the one Reality. In Self-Knowledge, the Self alone is the knower, knowing, and known, with no other instrument or means of knowledge.

The Self is the sole-existent Reality. Nothing apart from it is ever created. No other knower is ever born. There is no one to think, nothing to be thought of, and no thought created. Nonduality is the only Truth. May we abide ever in that Knowledge.

Thoughts always have for their content something objective—subtle or gross, abstract or more defined. There is no such thing as a nonobjective thought. The Self is never an object. Therefore, it is not possible to truly think of the Self. The Self is Reality, and Self-Knowledge alone is true knowledge. Therefore, thoughts deal solely with what is not real and hence not true knowledge.

The disciple approaches the Maharshi seeking to learn how to think of the Self. Why? It is because, in ignorance, one is accustomed to objective knowledge, which is actually ignorance, and assumes that what is conceived within the mind is real. In fact though, what is conceived in thought does not actually exist, while that which can never be conceived in thought actually alone exists. Because this is so, some wish to refer to the Self as "the unknown." However, by inquiry, one knows the Self by the Self; nor does anyone not know the Self for does anyone deny his own Existence? What could be more intimate than the Self? It is the best known. Moreover, there is nothing else to be known; nor is there any instrument of knowledge other than Consciousness; so the Self alone is known. Enlightened by Sri Adi Sankara, Suresvaracarya, in *Naishkarmyasiddhi* 2:105, says, "Only the destruction of avidya (ignorance, non-knowledge), is indeed, figuratively spoken of as the result. Knowing what was unknown before is not tenable since the Self is of the nature of Knowledge alone."

The Maharshi responds by declaring the self-luminosity of the Self. Consciousness requires no other light, no other means of knowing; it shines in its own light, and it undergoes no change and experiences no phases. Though referred to as the clear "Light of Consciousness" to express that it is clear Knowledge itself, the Self is not, and is not defined by, any of the mind's notions or images of darkness and light. The Self is the Reality, which is self-manifest. It exists, and its existence is self-existent, not dependent on anything else in order to be. It reveals itself to itself in the realization of the nonexistence of ignorance.

"Therefore, one should not think of it as this or as that." The Self is Being. It is not being this or that. It is Being alone; and in Being, there is an utter absence of ignorance.

To think of the Self as this or that is to superimpose the objective unreality upon the nonobjective Reality. It is to misidentify the forever-inconceivable Self, which is the vast, perfectly full Brahman, with what is merely imagination. Such is bondage. Therefore, one should not attempt to think of the Self. If one thinks that he will now commence to think of the Self, he will suppose himself to be one thing and the Self to be another, and then and there bondage appears. However much he thinks, the Self will not be known in that manner. Yet, if he turns his mind truly inward, he will then abandon such misidentification and come to know the Self as it is.

Meditation that consists of contemplation upon what is profound may be regarded as helpful in the course of spiritual practice, but it cannot substitute for meditation that consists of the actual inquiry to know the Self. To turn the mind inward so that it abandons its own notions, to so inquire so that Self-Knowledge is experienced, and not merely thought of, is essential in this inquiry. Therefore, in a passage in *Who am I?* that has parallels to this section of Self-inquiry, the Maharshi says, "To inquire 'Who am I that is in bondage?' and to know one's real nature is alone Liberation. To keep the mind constantly turned within and to abide thus in the Self is alone Atma-vichara, whereas dhyana consists in fervent contemplation of the Self as Sat-Chit-Ananda. Indeed, at some time, one will have to forget everything that has been learnt."

In meditation, the mind should lose its form. When the mind loses its form, its real nature and only existence is evident. That is the Self, which is nondual Consciousness. The form of the Self means the nature of the Self, as the Self has no defining form. The mind that is of the form of the Self is no mind at all. Thus it is said that the mind of the jnani is Brahman.

In the very center, as the quintessence of our Being, is Brahman directly experienced as the Self. It is not the ego, but the perfect, eternal Self, "I-I." That is known as the Heart. Thus, *Chandogya Upanishad* 8:3:3, "He, indeed, this Self, surely exists in the heart. Of that, this is, indeed, the explicit interpretation. It is in the heart; therefore, that is called the heart." Similarly, in the invocation of *Saddarsanam (Truth Revealed, Reality in Forty Verses)*, the Maharshi later stated, and Ganapati Muni translated into Sanskrit, "Free from thoughts, it exists, this inner Being, the Heart." (English translation by A. R. Natarjan.)

Ignorance is characterized by notions about the Self. Conceiving of more ideas about it will not eradicate the ignorance. What is necessary for the abolition of ignorance is the immediate Knowledge of the Self. How else is one to experience Self-Knowledge except by inquiring into the Self?

Therefore, without conceiving of the Self as this or that or in any manner whatsoever, and without conceiving of anything else, inquire, "Who am I?" and thus know the Self by the Self. It is Being, just Being, and not being this or that. It is simple Being alone. That alone is real. This is Self-Realization.

Whoever is so graced as to inquire into the Self, free of all conceptions about the Self, realizes the nondual Self, Brahman, and, free of the least trace of ignorance, abides as the sole-existent Self in infinite Wisdom and Bliss.

Om Sri Ramanarpanamastu
Om May this be an offering to Sri Ramana

32

Disciple: It was stated that Brahman is manifest as the Self in the form "I-I" in the heart. To facilitate an understanding of this statement, can it be still further explained?

The Maharshi: Is it not within the experience of all that during deep sleep, swoon, etc., there is no knowledge whatsoever, i.e., neither self-knowledge nor other-knowledge? Afterwards, when there is experience of the form "I have woken up from sleep" or "I have recovered from swoon"—is that not a mode of specific knowledge that has arisen from the aforementioned distinctionless state? This specific knowledge is called vijnana. This vijnana becomes manifest only as pertaining to either the Self or the not-self, and not by itself. When it pertains to the Self, it is called true knowledge, knowledge in the form of that mental mode whose object is the Self, or knowledge that has for its content the impartite (Self); and when it relates to the not-self, it is called ignorance. The state of this vijnana, when it pertains to the Self and is manifest as the form of the Self, is said to be the "I"-manifestation. This manifestation cannot take place as apart from the Real (i.e., the Self). It is this manifestation that serves as the mark for the direct experience of the Real. Yet, this by itself cannot constitute the state of being the Real. That, depending on which this manifestation takes place, is the basic Reality, which is also called prajnana. The Vedantic text "Prajnanam Brahma" teaches the same truth.

Know this as the purport of the scripture also. The Self, which is self-luminous and the witness of everything, manifests itself as residing in the vijnanakosa (sheath of the intellect). By the mental mode which is impartite, seize this Self as your goal and enjoy it as the Self.

Commentary:

Om Namo Bhagavate Sri Ramanaya

In order to further elucidate the nature of the Knowledge of the Self for the benefit of those seeking to penetrate into the mystery of their own Consciousness, Sri Bhagavan expounds upon the characteristics of vijnana and prajnana. Vijnana is a term employed in a variety of ways in different texts of Advaita Vedanta, but, in this case, it refers to knowledge that distinguishes, which is in keeping with the mention of the sheath of the intellect (vijnanamaya kosa) or intelligence. In as much as such appears and disappears and is an aspect of mental activity, it is to be negated as not being the Self and as being unreal by those inquiring to realize the Self. In as much as there is only one knower, who is of the nature of pure Consciousness, and who appears to be endowed with the capacity to turn inward to the Self, though in doing so all distinctions are lost, in essence, it is not other than that Self of pure Consciousness. When focused on that which is not the Self, it is the abode of delusion. When focused on the Self, it shines as knowledge. Yet, as the Self is eternally transcendent of all duality, and is conditionless and stateless, such knowledge is negated by the knowers of Truth. This all-transcendent Self, of the nature of nondual Consciousness, is itself the Supreme Knowledge. It is, therefore, called "Prajnana."

Profound spiritual thought, in the form of specific knowledge, may assist the aspirant, yet the final, real Knowledge is beyond thought. The former depends on the latter (Knowledge), the latter not on the former.

The Maharshi commences his explanation by drawing the disciple's mind to observe states such as deep sleep and swoon in which, in the absence of thought activity, there is no knowledge of other things or any thought about oneself. It is a state without distinctions. Upon one's exit from such states, specific knowledge, or relative awareness, arises. Or, it may be said that when this relative awareness arises, such manifests as the change of state. This specific knowledge, which has numerous modes, is termed vijnana.

When vijnana pertains to what is not the Self, it is of no benefit to the seeker of Self-Realization. Such is only ignorance. When vijnana is turned inward to contemplate the Self, the result is beneficial knowledge. It pertains to what is true and leads to the indivisible state. It manifests as a single-pointed focus upon the "I." The "I" is thus noticed and not overlooked, so its real nature can be discerned.

The "I" does not stand apart from the real Self. Since it pertains to one's identity, the "I" may be said to be the sign or mark for the experience of the Self. It is through inquiry into this "I" that the state of Realization is reached. The "I," the subtlest form of vijnana, rests upon the substrate of the basic Reality. That Reality, which depends on none, but on which all depend, which is not an "I" but is I, is Prajnana. Prajnana means Supreme Knowledge or Consciousness. The mahavakya of Vedanta, "Prajnanam Brahma" declares that the Consciousness, Supreme Knowledge, is Brahman.

Prajnana is not a function. It does not belong to anyone. It is the Self of all. It is not relative awareness, though there is no relative awareness apart from it. It is the Absolute. Brahman is, itself, the Supreme Knowledge. Supreme Knowledge is Consciousness. Consciousness is only one, is immutable, and is indivisible. So, the Realization of Supreme Knowledge cannot happen to anyone or to any mind, as such a one or mind does not exist to so attain. The Supreme Knowledge is not obtained or produced, is not the result of any transformation, and its Realization is not an event. Consciousness is, itself, the Knowledge of itself, which is absolute. Brahman alone knows itself and it, itself, is the

Knowledge of itself. This is Self-Knowledge, the Knowledge of Brahman, revealed by the Maharshi.

The Self is self-luminous and is never an object of knowledge or awareness. It is the solitary witness of all and the unknown knower of all that is known as declared by the *Kena Upanishad*. It appears as if residing in vijnanakosa, the sheath of the intellect or specific knowledge. In truth though, it is innately transcendent of that sheath. The Self is Prajnana; that is the sole knower, and vijnanakosa is inert with no capacity of its own to know.

The Maharshi states the direct path: with an undivided mind, or in the undivided mode, realize the Self alone to be the goal of spiritual practice and blissfully experience, as your own Self, your only true identity. The meditation of the undivided mode becomes the Realization that all is only of the undivided mode. Brahman is the undivided mode. The Self is only the undivided mode. The jiva is of the undivided mode. All the sheaths are only the undivided mode. The meditator, meditation, and the objects of meditation are all only the undivided mode. The mind is only the undivided mode. The five elements and the universe are only the undivided mode. Space is only the undivided mode. Time is only the undivided mode. Listening, reflection, and profound meditation are all only the undivided mode. Samadhi is only the undivided mode. The idea of the undivided mode is only the undivided mode. What is termed the "undivided mode" is only Brahman, the Self alone. Even thus, did that Supreme Self—Guru Ramana—as Rishi Ribhu declared in ancient times, reiterating the very teaching bequeathed to him from Siva Himself.

All this is the undivided Supreme Knowledge. There is nothing else to know. Meditating unswervingly on the Self, know the Self by the Self and enjoy the Bliss of the Self as the only Reality of yourself.

Whoever follows the trail of the "I," though it be vijnana, like a dog tracing its master by his scent, with the grace of the realized sages, realizes the Supreme Knowledge revealed by the wondrous all-knowing guru, Bhagavan Sri Ramana Maharshi and, abiding in the impartite state, ever enjoys infinite Wisdom and Bliss.

Om Sri Ramanarpanamastu
Om May this be an offering to Sri Ramana

33

Disciple: What is that which is called the inner worship or worship of the attributeless?

The Maharshi: In texts such as the *Ribhu Gita,* the worship of the attributeless has been elaborately explained (as a separate discipline). Yet, all disciplines such as sacrifice, charity, austerity, observance of vows, japa, yoga, and puja, are in effect, modes of meditation of the form "I am Brahman." So, in all the modes of discipline, one should see to it that one does not stray away from the thought "I am Brahman." This is the purport of the worship of the attributeless.

Commentary:
Om Namo Bhagavate Sri Ramanaya

Many are the aims and purposes attributed to outer forms and expressions of spiritual practice, such as the aspects of yoga previously mentioned, tapas, japa, vows, puja, etc. For one whose aim is Self-Realization, the inner significance of these is experienced, whether attended by the outer observances, or practices, or not. This inner significance is shown by the guru, through verbal instruction, silent example, or inner revelation. Whatever be the form of practice or worship, such is just a means to express or point the mind toward that which is attributeless.

Inner worship, or worship of the attributeless, is essential and brings perfect union with the Absolute. This worship has been explained in such texts as *Ribhu Gita* and Adi Sankara's *Nirguna Manasa Puja* and is referred to by *Tripura Rahasya* and numerous other scriptures. The essence is always abidance in identity with Brahman. That is the supreme form of worship, for there is not a trace of the ego or difference in it. In all forms of worship, if this essential essence of worship is maintained, the entire worship is elevated to the highest. The "thought of Brahman" here refers to the specific knowledge of "I am Brahman" being evident in one's experience as the unbroken thread at the center of, and connecting, all the flowers of practices and modes of worship in the mala (garland) of the life divine absorbed in Brahman.

When one offers in sacrifice, as in a yagna, one should see that the offering is Brahman, the offerer is Brahman, the priest is Brahman, the fire is Brahman, any murti present is Brahman, and I am Brahman—all is only Brahman alone. When charity is practiced, one should see that the donor is Brahman, the recipient is Brahman, what is given is Brahman, the giving is Brahman, and I am Brahman—all is only Brahman. When tapas (austerity) is performed, one should know the tapasvi (practitioner of tapas) is Brahman, the tapas is Brahman, the fruit of the tapas is Brahman, and I am Brahman—all is only Brahman. When one observes a vow, the one who vows, the vow itself, the result of the vow, the effort to maintain the vow, that presence in which the vow is made, and I, are all only Brahman. In japa, the mantra is only Brahman, the source of the mantra is only Brahman, the repetition is only Brahman, the result is only Brahman, and the one who practices is only Brahman. The name of God and praise of God refer to Brahman and are one's own names and praises. "I am Brahman" is the essence. Likewise in yoga, the yogi, the practice, the goal and the result are entirely Brahman. Brahman alone attains union (yoga) with Brahman alone, and I am that Brahman. In puja, the worshipper is Brahman, worshipping, which is Brahman, the Worshipped, which is only Brahman. That is the Self. The Self is alone truly the "I," and I am Brahman. Such is "worship of the attributeless."

In the Sanskrit *Ribhu Gita,* chapter seven deals with tarpana (libation of water for worship) and homa (worship with fire) in reference to the highest Knowledge of the Self. At the conclusion of chapter three of the scripture, Suta says in these three verses:

46. Internally, I shall perform worship to the One whose body is space by "Isavasya" and other mantras, by offering a seat and garments and praise, offering worship to the Isana

linga for the Supreme One, the Great, who is established in the midst of the primal cosmos, anointing one who cannot be wetted, offering garments to one who is clothed in space, offering sweet smelling flowers to the One who is without nose or smell or form or appearance,

47. offering lamps to One who is self-illumined, offering naivedya (consecrated cooked food) to One who is the ever-satisfied all-devourer, with circumambulations and prostrations to the One who strides over the worlds. In this, my authority is, indeed, the crest of the Vedas.

48. Those who know not offer worship by means of an endless parade of symbolism and with a mind set on rituals. Those who know, however, worship inwardly, in abstract meditation, their minds attuned to the prescribed injunctions. Yet, Isvara, though continuing to confuse the world, takes into His abode all who worship with various bhava-s and makes them transcendent in Knowledge.

The *Ribhu Gita* used by the Maharshi would most probably have been the Tamil *Ribhu Gita,* and it is this to which reference is made. According to B. V. Narasimha Swami, Sri Bhagavan wrote in Seshiar's notebook the gist of this portion of that scripture in some five or more pages. The relevant portion of the Tamil *Ribhu Gita* text appears in the latter portion of chapter 3:

27. How [is one] to invoke for worship (in a fixed place)
    the Supreme Siva
    Who is of the nature of sphurana (flashing,
        sparkling, breaking forth, vibrating)?
    How [is one] to offer a seat to the Supreme Siva
    Who is the substratum (base) of everything?
    How [is one] to offer water for washing the feet and
        other honors to the already pure One?
    How [is one] to bathe the Self-abiding One who can-
        not be wetted by anything?

How [is one] to cover with an offering of cloth
The Supreme One who is all-pervasive and clothed
  only in space?

28. How [is one] to put across the sacred thread
For the One who is beyond all prescribed castes and
  orders of life?
How [is one] to adorn with shining ornaments
The incorporeal, undifferentiated One?
How [is one] to anoint with sweet-smelling sandal
  paste
The One with no connections or attachments?
How [is one] to offer with fragrant flowers
The One who is devoid of any vasana-s (scent of
  anamnesis, tendency)?

29. How [is one] to offer, with love, incense and light to
  the One
Who is noseless and is Self-illumined?
How [is one] to offer food (naivedya) to the One
Who, in reality,
Is immersed in Bliss?
How [is one] to offer betels to the One
Who, Himself, indeed, delights all the worlds?
How [is one] to offer all other honors?

30. How [is one] to offer the camphor light
To the luminous Consciousness that reveals fire
  and such other (lights)?
How [is one] to circumambulate
Around the endless One?
How [is one] to fall in full prostration
In front of the ever nondual One?
How [is one] to praise with words
The One who is beyond the reach of the mind and
  words?

31. How [is one] to release to his usual abode, after
       worship,
    The One who pervades everything internal and
       external?
    Though such external worship with all these
       honors
    Is inappropriate for the Lord (Isvara),
    Listen son! with attention and interest,
    To the worship of the changeless Sambhu (bestower
       of happiness), Existence-Knowledge-Bliss,
    By internal bhavana (conviction) as expounded
    In the knowledgeable Vedanta texts.

32. The conviction that there is no such thing as maya
       (illusion)
    And [that] I remain as the delusionless Supreme
       Siva
    Is the avahana (invocation).
    The conviction that I am the pure Supreme Siva,
       changeless and abiding in Himself,
    Is the offering of a spotless asana (seat).
    The conviction that I am not affected by good or bad
       accretions
    Consequent on connections of the mind
    Is the offering of water for padya (the washing of
       the feet).

33. Renunciation of the longstanding, widespread, and
       fickle avidya (ignorance)
    Is the respectful libation to the linga of the Self.
    The conviction that all will drink
    Of the drops of the unimpeded shower
    Of the Bliss that is the Supreme Siva
    Is the offering of achamana (a sip of water).
    Hear further, son!
    The mode of performing abhiseka (the ablution).

34. The contemplation that all the worlds are moist
    With the perfectly full, delightful rain that is I

And I am the unblemished Brahman
That cannot become wet with the water of action is
the effective ablution.
The determination that I am the perfect fullness
That cannot be covered in the least by anything else
Is the appropriate offering of a garment
To the linga (symbol of Siva) of the Supreme Self.

35. The meditation that I am the Supreme Brahman,
The power that wears the three strands of the three
guna-s (qualities), which constitute the world,
Is the offering of the sacred thread to the linga of
the Supreme Self.
Determining that I am the Self,
Which is incorporeal and totally devoid of all
distinguishing marks,
Is the offering of ornaments.
The contemplation that I am the power entirely
pervading the world,
With various scents (of past impressions, vasana-s),
is the offering of sandal paste.

36. Renouncing the vritti-s (modes) that are the
consequences of the three guna-s (qualities)
Constitutes the offering of rice grains to the
primordial linga.
Rejecting the threefold division of "preceptor," "I,"
and "Isvara (Lord),"
Is the offering of bilva leaves.
Avoiding the bad odor of the vasana-s (impressions
of the past)
Is the waving of incense.
The constant bhavana (conviction) that I am the
Supreme Siva,
Without qualities and Self-illumined, is the offering
of light.

37. The understanding that I am the several crores of
     universes
    Is the food offering to the Supreme Siva.
    The undivided mode that is the enjoyment of the
     changeless Brahman-Bliss
    Constitutes the offering of vyanjana (seasonings).
    The incessant cleaning with Knowledge
    Of the sticky, polluted remains,
    Called fundamental, fickle ignorance,
    Constitutes the offering of water for the washing
     of hands.

38. Renouncing the attachment to sensual pleasures
    Is the offering of tambula (betal packs).
    The pure Knowledge of Brahman,
    Which dispels the darkness of ignorance,
    Is the glowing camphor offering.
    The perception that all that appears as multiplicity
     is the one Brahman
    Is the offering of a pure flower garland,
    Oh pure one! to the Supreme Siva linga, the mass of
     Bliss.

39. The contemplation that I am the perfectly full,
     blissful Self
    Is the scattering of flowers in worship.
    The contemplation that the universe with its
     myriad activities revolves around me
    Constitutes the prescribed circumambulation.
    The contemplation that all will ever bow to me,
    And I shall never bow to anyone,
    Ever constitutes the bow
    To the great linga of the Self.

40. The thought that there is no trace
    Of name and form in me, who am the universe,
    Constitutes the singing of the exalted names,
    Which is a prescribed feature of the worship of the
     Supreme.

The contemplation that there is no need
For any deed for me in this world
Constitutes other honors to be extended
In worship by the mind.

41. The absorption in meditation,
Rid of all delusions of the mind and distractions,
Constitutes the release of the linga, the Supreme
    Siva without parts,
Back to the usual abode.
One who thus performs this pure worship
Even once as told in Vedanta
Will remove vasana-s (past impressions, tendencies)
    and all ajnana (ignorance) and sorrow
And attain the great Bliss of Liberation.

Whoever, adhering to the sacred instruction of the Maharshi, worships the Attributeless, never straying from the Knowledge of identity, experiences Brahman everywhere and at all times and in the endless space-like temple of Brahman, as Brahman itself, abides in infinite Wisdom and Bliss.

Om Sri Ramanarpanamastu
Om May this be an offering to Sri Ramana

34

Disciple: What are the eight limbs of knowledge (jnana-ashtanga)?

The Maharshi: The eight limbs are those which have been already mentioned, viz. yama, niyama, etc., but differently defined.

Of these—
(1) Yama:—This is controlling the aggregate of sense-organs, realizing the defects that are present in the world consisting of the body, etc.

(2) Niyama:—This is maintaining a stream of mental modes that relate to the Self and rejecting the contrary

modes. In other words, it means love that arises uninterruptedly for the supreme Self.

(3) Asana:—That with the help of which constant meditation on Brahman is made possible with ease is asana.

(4) Pranayama:—Rechaka (exhalation) is removing the two unreal aspects of name and form from the objects constituting the world, the body, etc., puraka (inhalation) is grasping the three real aspects, existence, consciousness and bliss, which are constant in those objects, and kumbhaka is retaining those aspects thus grasped.

(5) Pratyahara:—This is preventing name and form that have been removed from re-entering the mind.

(6) Dharana:—This is making the mind stay in the heart without straying outward and realizing that one is the Self itself, which is Existence-Consciousness-Bliss.

(7) Dhyana:—This is meditation of the form "I am only pure Consciousness." That is, after leaving aside the body, which consists of five sheaths, one inquires 'Who am I?', and, as a result of that, one stays as "I" which shines as the Self.

(8) Samadhi:—When the "I"-manifestation also ceases, there is (subtle) direct experience. This is samadhi.

For the pranayama, etc., detailed here, the disciplines such as asana, etc., mentioned in connection with yoga, are not necessary. The limbs of knowledge may be practiced at all places and at all times. Of yoga and knowledge, one may follow whichever is pleasing to one, or both, according to circumstances. The great teachers say that forgetfulness is the root of all evil and is death for those who seek release; so one should rest the mind in one's Self and should never forget the Self; this is the aim. If the mind is controlled, all else can be controlled. The distinction between yoga with eight limbs and knowledge with eight limbs has been set forth elaborately in the sacred texts, so only the substance of this teaching has been given here.

Commentary:

Om Namo Bhagavate Sri Ramanaya

Earlier, Sri Bhagavan mentioned an eight-limbed path of Knowledge (Jnana). These eight limbs, though bearing names common with yoga, are in accord with Advaita Vedanta. The disciplines of yoga and the restrictions of yoga in regard to time, place, etc. do not pertain to this path of jnana, though one on the path of jnana is not prohibited from observing the disciplines of yoga. However, what is essential in order to overcome the forgetfulness of one's true nature, which alone is the cause of suffering and which "is death for those who seek Liberation," is to keep one's aim solely on the Self.

The Maharshi says, as recorded in the notebook, "Forgetting the Self is stated to be death," alluding to the *Sanatsujatiyam,* which states in verse four near the commencement of the text, in the words of Sanatsujata,

मोहो मृत्युः सम्मतो यः कवीनाम् ।
प्रमादं वै मृत्युमहं ब्रवीमि सदाप्रमादममृतत्वं ब्रवीमि ॥

moho mṛtyuḥ sammato yaḥ kavīnām |
pramādaṁ vai mṛtyumaham bravīmi
sadāpramādamamṛtatvaṁ bravīmi ||

"Delusion is death is the concurrence of the wise. Inadvertence (carelessness, heedlessness, being thrown into confusion) is death, I say. Eternal awareness (being ever attentive) is immortality, I say." In His commentary thereon, Adi Sankara reveals that delusion is false knowledge (mithyajnanam) consisting of the ignorant misidentification of what is other than, or not, the Self with the Self. The inadvertence is the "death" consisting of the imaginary differentiation from the innately immortal true Being, which is the Self. The egoless, difference-less Knowledge of the Self, which is the self-effulgence of Consciousness without any misidentification, is the perfection of innate immortality.

That is unconditional Bliss, which is self-revealed as one's perpetual experience and as identical with Being-Consciousness upon the destruction of the misidentification constituting ignorance, for such ignorance is alone the cause of suffering.

If it is essential to overcome forgetfulness of one's true nature, and one should rest the mind in one's Self and never forget the Self, how is such non-forgetfulness attained? How is one to rest his mind in the Self? Ignorance does not belong to the Self, which is of the nature of unalloyed Consciousness. Inquiry that dissolves the false assumption of the individual who could forget the true nature of Self is the way to such attainment of the perpetual, uninterrupted Knowledge of the Self. The Self can no more forget itself than Being can cease to be. If the mind is turned inward, which means to inquire and thereby relinquish the mind's own imaginings, it loses its form, and all that remains of it is pure Consciousness. Such is said to be a mind resting in the Self. In practice, the effort is applied to the inquiry to know the Self. Such inquiry is primarily a negation of what is not the Self, as the Self is nonobjective. The objective outlook being abandoned, non-forgetfulness of the Self is natural.

Yoga is said to be control of the mind or control of the modes of the mind. The mind and its modes are of the nature of illusory differentiation. Jnana reveals the nonexistence of a separate mind and the reality of undifferentiated Consciousness. Therefore, Jnana is lauded as the best form of control, or mastery, of the mind.

Sri Ramana says that he is stating only the gist of the limbs of jnana as they are dealt with elaborately in other texts. Though not divided into eight, the same aspects of jnana in the parlance of yoga are expounded by Adi Sankara in *Aparoksanubhuti,* in fifteen-steps reiterating the same nondual fifteen step jnana-yoga expounded in *Tejobindupanishad,* which contains the instructions given by Siva to Kumara and by Ribhu to Nidagha.

In jnana, yama is "realizing the defects of the world inclusive of the body" and thereby "controlling the aggregate of sense-organs." What are the defects? The world and the body are defects because they are transient, are subject to constant change, are limited, are composed of parts apart from which they do not exist and hence are empty names, are dependent upon the senses and waking state of the mind even to appear, have a creation or birth and a destruction or death, are not the source of happiness, and cause bondage when there is attachment to them. The same is true of the senses themselves. Nonattachment to the senses is the best control, easily attained when one perceives their defects. Nonattachment is wisdom and bliss.

In jnana, niyama is the focus of the mind, like the steady flow of a stream, upon the Self. It includes the rejection of notions concerning the non-Self because they pertain to the unreal and are not productive of blissful wisdom. In essence, it is the deep love for the Supreme Self, the abode of perfect bliss. One who practices this jnana niyama remains fixed on the Self with an all-consuming fascination and is completely detached from all. He discerns modes of thinking that are of a delusive nature and abandons them entirely because of his love for the Self. If that love is uninterrupted, even the ideas about what is not the Self are not conjured up. This state of love is blissfully wise.

In jnana, asana is said to be that with the help of which constant meditation on Brahman is made possible with ease. To be seated in the Self is the supreme asana. To abide as that which is the non-dual support of the entire universe is the limitless asana. To be still, unmoved by illusion, is the sublime asana. To have the mind steady, whether the body is moving or not, is the transcendent asana. Firmness in inquiry is the correct asana. The destruction of the ego and body misidentifications is the smiling-corpse-like asana. To abide without misidentification with the body is the bodiless asana of "jnana that can be practiced in any place or posture," as stated in Gambhiram Seshayya's notebook. If one feels his stand is steadfastly upon or in the Truth, he is practicing the jnana asana, which is to be seated in blissful wisdom.

In jnana, pranayama has its own details. Rechaka (exhalation) is defined as the removal of the two unreal aspects from the objects constituting the world, inclusive of the body. The unreal aspects are the form and the name. If form is removed from anything and even its name, or the idea of it, is no more, what remains is its real substance: Existence. In this jnana rechaka, the unreal is "exhaled," and all is known in its true Existence, which is Brahman. Puraka (inhalation) is defined as the grasping or comprehending of the three real aspects of the objects from which rechaka removed the unreal name and form. The real aspects are Existence, Consciousness, and Bliss. All that is is only Existence. All that is is only Consciousness. Existence and Consciousness are one and the same. Wherever Existence-Consciousness is is also Bliss. Neither Bliss nor the others are attributes of either the objects or of each other. That which is, conceived as an object or not, is only That, which is Being-Consciousness-Bliss, and this three-fold term is intended to indicate the nature of the one, indivisible Reality. Kumbhaka (retention) is defined as retaining those aspects thus grasped, that is, to remain firm in the Knowledge of Being-Consciousness-Bliss. This jnana pranayama is the one to be practiced for those who wish to experience wisdom and bliss with every breath.

In jnana, pratyahara is defined as preventing the recurrence of name and form after they have been eradicated. Name and form are imagined by the mind and appear within the mind. There are no names and forms outside of the mind; all that is within the mind. This imagination is done away with by Knowledge of what really exists as related under pranayama. The same Knowledge that discerns the unreal as unreal and recognizes the real as real will prevent the recurrence of the unreal illusion. Ignorance is created by oneself and not by external causes. Belief in it as if it were knowledge, as if it were real, maintains it. When Knowledge born of inquiry destroys the ignorance by showing it to be only ignorance and hence unreal, who would cling to it or conjure it up again? Consistency in this Knowledge and the cutting off of the possibility of future delusion is this jnana pratyahara, which is wise and blissful.

In jnana, dharana is defined as making the mind stay in the heart without outward straying and realizing one's identity as the Self, of the nature of Existence-Consciousness-Bliss. If the mind turns inward, abandoning as false its own notions, it relinquishes its own form and abides in the Heart, the quintessence of Being. Straying outward is the illusory projection of the reality of Being-Consciousness-Bliss upon thoughts, which in themselves are unreal. With the superimposition of Being, the mind, thoughts, and the content of thoughts are erroneously assumed to be real. With the superimposition of Consciousness upon thoughts, the mind is considered to be a knowing entity, notions are considered to be valid knowledge, and the content, or objects, of thought is considered as something known. When Bliss is superimposed on thought, emotions, moods, and attachments appear. When the mind stays in the Heart, all of the superimpositions cease, the unreal things vanish, and the Reality of Existence-Consciousness-Bliss remains unveiled. One should realize oneself to be this Existence-Consciousness-Bliss alone. The Self is only That. This is the jnana dharana conducive to concentrated wisdom and bliss.

In jnana, dhyana is defined as the meditation upon "I am only pure Consciousness." The Maharshi gives further clarity by declaring it to be inquiry which, casting aside the five sheaths, questions "Who am I?" thus causing one to abide as the ever-shining real "I," the Self. The five sheaths, previously described, represent the veils covering the Self, making the Self appear as a limited form. When one inquires "Who am I?" one ceases to be veiled with the five sheaths. Starting with the body, the misidentifications are destroyed. If one then further inquires, the ever-present true I, unalloyed Consciousness, is realized as one's own Being. This jnana dhyana, which causes one to realize the Truth of the Self, is the most excellent of meditations, being of the nature of unsullied, unveiled wisdom and bliss.

The eighth and final aspect of the path of jnana described herein is samadhi. Sri Bhagavan defines samadhi as the direct experience when the "I" manifestation ceases. It is complete, irreversible absorption in the Self. The "I-I" state is Being the Self, and that, in truth, is Self-Realization, or Self-Knowledge. It is called direct experience because there is neither experiencer nor experienced, neither realizer nor something realized. It is the natural and only real state. It is the utter absence of the ego. There is, then, no one to be bound; nor is there one who is liberated. The timeless Self alone is. This samadhi is itself pure wisdom and bliss.

Whoever ascends the path of jnana as revealed by Sri Bhagavan abides in the highest, is liberated from all illusion, and, expelling all ignorance and retaining true Knowledge, realizes the nature of the Self to be Being-Consciousness-Bliss and, by virtue of the ideal meditation—inquiry as to "Who am I?"—is absorbed in the perfect, timeless Samadhi of infinite Wisdom and Bliss.

Om Sri Ramanarpanamastu
Om May this be an offering to Sri Ramana

35

Disciple: Is it possible to practice at the same time the pranayama belonging to yoga and the pranayama pertaining to knowledge?

The Maharshi: So long as the mind has not been made to rest in the heart, either through absolute retention (kevala-kumbhaka) or through inquiry, rechaka, puraka, etc., are needed. Hence the pranayama of yoga is to be practiced during training, and the other pranayama may be practiced always. Thus, both may be practiced. It is enough if the yogic pranayama is practiced until skill is gained in absolute retention.

Commentary:

Om Namo Bhagavate Sri Ramanaya

The disciple evidences a desire to practice the pranayama of yoga. The guru knows what is best and when and how to do it. If, after the instruction bestowed by the Maharshi, the disciple were ripe to throw himself entirely into the direct path of pure, nondual jnana, this question would not have arisen. Yet the guru is compassion incarnate. Simultaneously, he urges the disciple to plunge inward and see the immediacy of the true Self, and, while Himself abiding as the Eternal, he patiently guides the disciple according to his temperament.

With pranayama and all the other limbs, the yoga approach can be practiced sporadically, that is in sessions of training, but the jnana approach is for continuous, unceasing practice and abidance in the Self.

Whoever catches so much as a glimpse of the guru's grace, brimming with divine love and compassion, melts to the very bones in devotion, is enabled to follow the right path as revealed by the guru, and, with the ego humbled and dissolved, finds himself, by grace, dwelling in infinite Wisdom and Bliss.

Om Sri Ramanarpanamastu

Om May this be an offering to Sri Ramana

36

Disciple: Why should the path to release be differently taught? Will it not create confusion in the minds of aspirants?

The Maharshi: Several paths are taught in the Vedas to suit the different grades of qualified aspirants. Yet, since release is but the destruction of mind, all efforts have for their aim the control of mind. Although the modes of meditation may appear to be different from one another, in the end, all of them become one. There is no need to doubt this. One may adopt that path which suits the maturity of one's mind.

The control of prana, which is yoga, and the control of mind, which is jnana—these are the two principal means for the destruction of mind. To some, the former may appear easy, and to others the latter. Yet, jnana is like subduing a turbulent bull by coaxing it with green grass, while yoga is like controlling through the use of force. Thus, the wise ones say: of the three grades of qualified aspirants, the highest reach the goal by making the mind firm in the Self through determining the nature of the Real by Vedantic inquiry and by looking upon one's self and all things as of the nature of the Real; the mediocre, by making the mind stay in the heart through kevalakumbhaka and meditating for a long time on the Real; and the lowest grade, by gaining that state in a gradual manner through breath-control, etc.

The mind should be made to rest in the heart until the destruction of the "I"-thought, which is of the form of ignorance, residing in the heart. This itself is jnana; this alone is dhyana also. The rest are a mere digression of words, digression of the texts. Thus the scriptures proclaim. Therefore, if one gains the skill of retaining the mind in one's Self through some means or other, one need not worry about other matters.

The great teachers also have taught that the devotee is greater than the yogins and that the means to release is devotion, which is of the nature of reflection on one's own Self.

Thus, it is the path of realizing Brahman that is variously called Dahara-vidya, Brahma-vidya, Atma-vidya, etc. What more can be said than this? One should understand the rest by inference.

The scriptures teach in different modes. After analysing all these modes, the great ones declare this to be the shortest and the best means.

Commentary:

Om Namo Bhagavate Sri Ramanaya

The disciple raises a question about the variety of paths, wondering does such serve to confuse the minds of aspirants. The Maharshi replies that the variety, found even in the Veda-s, is to meet the variety of temperaments or abilities of aspirants. The paths, though, have one aim: the destruction of mind, which is Liberation. Efforts are made to direct the mind inward in order to obliterate illusion and suffering. The paths share this common aim and are selected by seekers according to the maturity of their minds.

Sri Bhagavan then gives a critique of yoga in the light of jnana, emphasizing the naturalness and height of jnana and the use of force and inferiority or slowness of yoga. To control a bull through force is arduous, and the results may only be temporary. To subdue a bull by coaxing it with green grass will pacify it and cause it to cheerfully oblige you in a consistent manner. He who sets himself within a view that his mind is his enemy must strive hard to conquer it and in the end must relinquish that view, fraught as it is with dualism. He, though, who, pursuing jnana, perceives what the mind most wants—the peace and bliss of the Self—makes no enemy of the mind, but wisely guides it home to its vast, blissful source, and, being free of duality, finds lasting peace.

They who pursue the inquiry of Vedanta establish their minds in the Self by discerning Reality. They determine what is real and find it to be the Self, negating as "neti, neti" (not this, not this) all that is not the Self. They look at themselves and all as being of the nature of the one Reality. This is the glorious path to the most exalted state.

Utilizing techniques of prolonged meditation, retention of breath, restraining oneself while maintaining solitude, etc., is considered a mediocre approach, though the aim is still to make the mind stay in the Heart. The lowest approach is the attempt to gradually induce that state by manipulation of prana through breath control and similar methods, often physical practices, with their inherent limitations.

Sri Bhagavan straightforwardly describes the simple, pristine path: destroy the "I"-notion, which is the primal ignorance and the source of all delusion, so that the vast space of the Heart, one's Being, is not cluttered or veiled by the ego. This is jnana, or Knowledge, and true meditation (dhyana). All the rest of the practices, meditations, and knowledge so-called, even that found in spiritual texts, is mere digression from the immediate presence of the real Self. Scriptures such as *Yoga Vasishtha* and *Bhagavad Gita* declare this to be so. One need not concern oneself with a variety of spiritual matters; rather by one's dissolution of the mind in the Self by whatever means are best for him, he reaches the desired, and destined, goal.

The great masters have declared the devotee to be greater, that is, in a higher state, than the one who pursues yoga as it has been defined. The greatness of such devotion is proclaimed by Sri Krisna in the twelfth chapter of the *Bhagavad Gita* as well as elsewhere, such as 10:10, 9:29, 9:22, and 6:47. Why is this so? The devotee may surrender all and thus efface all duality. The devotee can surrender any claim to the mind, and he is then free and at peace, without a bull to tame as he has made it over to Sri Bhagavan, who is the real owner and perfect "cowherd," the one who pulls away all ignorance and illusion. B. V. Narasimha Swami says that the Maharshi then pointed specifically to *Bhagavad Gita* 6:47, which states,

योगिनामपि सर्वेषां मद्गतेनान्तरात्मना ।
श्रद्धावान् भजते यो मां स मे युक्ततमो मतः ॥

yogināmapi sarveṣāṁ madgatenāntarātmanā |
śraddhāvān bhajate yo māṁ sa me yuktatamo mataḥ ||

"Of all yogins, he who, with faith, worships Me with his inner Self abiding (absorbed) in Me, he is deemed by Me as the most devout (steadfast)." So, of all those striving for union with God, the one who has lost his separate individuality, is regarded as abiding in the holiest state, for nothing remains of him but God. That is the steady Self-abidance, which is Union without division. Thus, in *Reality in Forty Verses*, the Maharshi says (verses 20 and 21): "Seeing God without seeing the Self who sees is only a mental image. Only he who has seen himself has seen God, since he has lost his individuality, and nothing remains but God. If it be asked, 'What is the meaning of the old scriptural texts that speak of seeing oneself as seeing God?' the reply is how, being one, can one see oneself? And if one cannot see oneself, how is one to see God?' Only by being swallowed up by God."

The Maharshi declares that devotion is said to be defined by the sages as reflection on one's own Self. There is nothing higher or more direct than such a path. By this path one realizes the Self. Self-Realization is the blissful wisdom known as Dahara-vidya, which is the Knowledge that is fine, according to *Chandogya Upanishad* and Sri Adi Sankara's commentary thereon (following parts six and seven, which deal with the knowledge of "That you are" and Existence is Brahman respectively, the Upanishad in part eight speaks of the city of Brahman, the center of which is the heart, within which is that which is dahara, small; Adi Sankara comments that this description is intended for those who are incapable of realizing the Knowledge expounded in the previous two parts and that, though the space in the heart is spoken of as dahara, or small, it contains all within itself), or the Knowledge of the God in the cave of the Heart as described in *Collected Works of Ramana Maharshi* (p. 280, 3rd edition 1968); Brahma-vidya, which is Knowledge of Brahman; and Atma-vidya, which is Knowledge of the Self. Other names are also given to it, yet no matter what they may be, that egoless state is always Being's own non-conceptual Knowledge of itself.

In the discrimination as to which is the best path, no more need be said. By inference, one can understand and arrive at the answer as to what is the direct, most efficacious path. Discussing the paths of others, in itself, is of no importance. What is important is to arrive at a settled conclusion as to what is best for liberation for oneself.

In the original notebook, a passage, unassigned to a particular time, ascribed to the Maharshi, appears that is certainly pertinent to the instruction contained in this chapter: "All paths meet in realizing the Self. If the mind wanders, we must at once realize, 'We are not the body,' and inquire, 'Who am I?' and the mind must be brought back to realize the Self. Thus, all evils are destroyed, and happiness is revealed." From this instruction from the greatest of rishis, we comprehend that the ultimate goal of any spiritual practice is Self-Realization. Therefore, since Self-Realization consists of egoless Self-Knowledge, the greater the scope of ego-loss and the more there is this essential Knowledge, the more fruitful the spiritual practice is. Maya is the delusion of the mind, and it wanders in its own imagination. For liberation from such, one must know that the body is not the Self and inquire deeply. With such deep inquiry, the mind is brought back from its meanderings in its own delusions, and, thus losing the forms it had assumed, is absorbed in the Self. Thus are all sufferings destroyed, dependent as they are upon the bondage composed of misidentification. The revelation of Being is that of Bliss, since they are one and the same thing. As the Maharshi has stated at another time, the revealing of the Self, or Being, which is ever there, is the one way to recover the Bliss that was never lost.

The scriptures are vast and contain numberless teachings to meet the needs of numberless aspirants. The great sages, with full Knowledge born of direct experience and a thorough comprehension of the scriptures, have already pointed out the clearest, most direct path to Self-Realization.

Whoever has full faith in what the Maharshi has thus revealed here will pursue the direct path free of dualisms and, full of devotion, will attain experience of the Truth, even as the ancient sages did, and thus abide in infinite Wisdom and Bliss.

Om Sri Ramanarpanamastu

Om May this be an offering to Sri Ramana

37

Disciple: By practicing the disciplines taught above, one may get rid of the obstacles that are in the mind, viz., ignorance, doubt, error, etc., and thereby attain quiescence of mind. Yet, there is one last doubt. After the mind has been resolved in the heart, there is only Consciousness shining as the plenary reality. When thus the mind has assumed the form of the Self, who is there to enquire? Such inquiry would result in Self-worship. It would be like the story of the shepherd searching for the sheep that was all the time on his shoulders!

The Maharshi: The jiva itself is Siva; Siva Himself is the jiva. It is true that the jiva is no other than Siva. When the grain is hidden inside the husk, it is called paddy; when it is de-husked, it is called rice. Similarly, so long as one is bound by karma one remains a jiva; when the bond of ignorance is broken, one shines as Siva, the Deity. Thus declares a scriptural text. Accordingly, the jiva, which is mind, is in reality the pure Self, but, forgetting this truth, it imagines itself to be an individual soul and gets bound in the shape of mind. So, its search for the Self, which is itself, is like the search for the sheep by the shepherd. But still, the jiva, which has forgotten itself, will not become the Self through mere mediate knowledge. By the impediment caused by the residual impressions gathered in previous births, the jiva forgets again and again its identity with the Self and gets deceived, identifying itself with the body, etc. Will a person become a high officer by merely looking at him? Is it not by steady effort in that direction that he could become a highly placed officer? Similarly, the jiva, which is in bondage through mental identification with the body, etc., should put forth effort in the form of reflection on the Self, in a gradual and sustained manner, and, when thus the mind gets destroyed, the jiva would become the Self.

The reflection on the Self that is thus practised constantly will destroy the mind and, thereafter, will destroy itself like the stick that is used to kindle the cinders burning a corpse. It is this state that is called release.

Commentary:

Om Namo Bhagavate Sri Ramanaya

The disciple's initial comments show that he has grasped the importance of Sri Ramana's teaching. The question involves confusion regarding the mind's disappearance in the perfectly full Consciousness and the place of inquiry in relation to Self-Knowledge.

Sri Bhagavan, who is none other than Siva himself, declares the Truth: the jiva is, itself, Siva. The individual is no individual at all, but only Siva. Siva is the Supreme Good, the Auspicious Absolute. Siva is that which destroys all illusion and remains itself as the residuum of pure, homogeneous, imperishable Being. There is no existence to the jiva but Siva. Siva plus bondage, as manifesting through the karma-s, appears as jiva. When the bondage, which is only ignorance, is destroyed, what appeared as the jiva shines as Siva. This is alluded to in *Skandhopanishad, Atmasakshatkara, Ribhu Gita,* other Saivite works, and by Sri Adi Sankara in several of his writings.

The mind is nothing other than the jiva. The jiva is nothing other than the Self. The Self is, itself, Siva. If the Truth is forgotten—and what else is ignorance but forgetfulness of one's true nature—the individual (jiva) is imagined as one's self, and it is the jiva that becomes bound in its own outgrowth, the mind. The Self does not become so bound; the jiva does. So, one illusion becomes bound in another. To be free of illusion and bondage, one must seek and find oneself.

The search for oneself is like the man searching for his sheep while it rests on his shoulders the whole time. He is oblivious to it. If only he discovers how what he is searching for is present with him the whole time, his search is ended, as he has recovered what he never really lost. So it is with the Self. Who else is present the entire time? This is similar to the story of the tenth man cited by Sri Ramana in *Forty Verses on Reality* and like the case of the woman who sought the jewel that she thought was missing while it hung around her neck all the while. As for the jiva and Siva, it is like the case of the wooden elephant: at first one sees the elephant and not the wood; later, with correct understanding, one sees the wood and no elephant, realizing that what was thought to be the elephant was only wood ever. Or it is like the rope and the snake; what is imagined to be a snake is realized to be a rope only without the least trace of a snake as soon as imagination is relinquished in the light of Knowledge. Similarly, the jiva is, in truth, only the Self. The Self alone is real, and the jiva is not.

The forgetfulness of the Self is enhanced by vasana-s, the tendencies or impressions that deceive one about the real nature of the Self and cause one to confound oneself with the body. The seeker may not remember when the vasana-s began. It is not relevant, for their destruction is alone what is needed. In the end, one discovers that they had no real beginning, for how can the unreal have a real beginning?

The mind's illusion will not be destroyed except by intense, persevering effort. Sri Bhagavan emphatically declares the need for such effort. Self-Realization is the effortless state, for it is of the nature of innate Being. Practice involves effort, the intensity of which has its source in the same Self. The effort of practice is not an attempt to create the real Self, for it is ever existent and beyond causality, but it is for the purpose of the destruction of illusion. Illusion is due to ignorance, and clear Knowledge of the Self alone destroys it. The practice of Knowledge is Self-inquiry. As long as there is an impediment to one's freedom, disturbance to one's peace, or limitation to one's happiness, one must strive with utmost intensity to realize the Self, like a man underwater with all effort attempting to rise above the surface to obtain air.

The emphasis on intensity of practice by the Maharshi and the insufficiency of mere verbal or mental "knowledge," bears a striking resemblance to Sri Adi Sankara's *Vivekacudamani,* verse 66 (verse 64 in some editions),

अकृत्वा शत्रुसंहारमगत्वाखिलभूश्रियम् ।
राजाहमिति शब्दान्नो राजा भवितुमर्हति ॥

akṛtvā śatrusaṁhāramagatvākhilabhūśriyam |
rājāhamiti śabdānno rājā bhavitumarhati ||

which may be translated as: "Not having completely destroyed the enemies, not having the wealth of the whole earth, one is not entitled to (is not able to) become a king by the mere words, thus, 'I am the king.'" Similarly, verse 65 (63 in some editions),

अकृत्वा दृश्यविलयमज्ञात्वा तत्त्वमात्मनः ।
ब्रह्मशब्दैः कुतो मुक्तिरुक्तिमात्रफलैर्नृणाम् ॥

akṛtvā dṛśyavilayamajñātvā tattvamātmanaḥ |
brahmaśabdaiḥ kuto muktiruktimātraphalairnṛṇām ||

which may be translated as: "Not having brought about the complete dissolution of the seen, not having known the Truth of the Self, from where (how) is Liberation by a great many words? It is nothing but a sentence (utterance), the results of words."

If practice is intense and consistent, the mind's illusions, inclusive of the illusion of "a mind," will be completely destroyed, like straw before a blazing fire. The ego and its accretions are but a corpse. Inquiry is the fiery practice. The meditation "Who am I?" is the stick used to kindle or stir the pyre. Its form is destroyed in the process. No one need jettison the inquiry at any time. One simply inquires, and, upon the vanishing of all ignorance, the means to Knowledge will also automatically vanish in the vast expanse of the peace of the space-like Self. This is Release, or Liberation.

In the notebook of Gambhiram Seshayya, B. V. Narasimha Swami says that the Maharshi is quoted as declaring: "The quest of the Self is really like a man searching for a goat upon his shoulder, but at the time of the search, the jiva or mind does not know or realize yet that he is himself the Atman that he seeks; hence the search continues until he discovers the goat upon himself. But to make this discovery takes a long time. There are vasana-s developed from time immemorial by reason of which the Self identifies itself with the body. These have to be constantly rubbed off by the recollection, "I am not the body." Only after this are the vasana-s conquered and the Self realized. This inquiry about the nature of the Self is itself a mental operation, but it destroys the mind just like the stick used in lighting the funeral pyre is itself destroyed after it has set fire to the pyre and the corpse."

Thus is shown the importance of making one's vision nonobjective, for it is one's own Self that is sought. Seeking continues until one realizes this Self. If the mind is turned outward, the search is in the unreal world conjured up by one's own mind and is fruitless. If the mind is turned inward, the search is spiritual, which is fruitful. If inwardness is fully pursued, the spiritual search is one for Self-Knowledge, the means for which is Self-inquiry. The mind alone does not know the Self, for the Self, of the nature of pure Consciousness, can possess no ignorance. The mind, or jiva, inquiring into itself in search of the Self, loses its assumed form, and the nondual Self alone remains. Though the Self and its Realization are timeless, for spiritual practice that thoroughly eliminates all tendencies of ignorance, time may be required. When the liberation from the misidentification with the body and such is complete, with recurrence of ignorance impossible, the Self is said to be realized. Knowledge of the Self is by the Self, itself; nothing else can do so. The mind, senses, etc., have no knowing power of their own and can neither know themselves nor the Self. The Real comprehends itself. The unreal cannot do so, for it does not exist. In practice, which is here addressed by the Maharshi because of his boundless compassion for all those struggling within the illusory samsara, it seems as if the inquiry starts at a mental level, such as with the thought "Who am I?" and is involved in resolving the tendencies of the mind. Moreover, the Self, itself, has neither ignorance nor inquiry, so, in explanation, the inquiry is said to be by and for the mind. The profound significance, though, of "Who am I?" is utterly mind-transcendent, and that which discerns the notions constituting the vasana-s is, itself, no notion within the mind at all. Therefore, what to the aspirant appears as an inward motion of the mind destroys, by its illimitable light, the darkness of all delusion, including the notion of an existent mind. That which remains is neither mind nor body, has neither form nor motion, and is ever free of any trace of delusion. This inquiry is a liberating blessing, and He who revealed it is grace itself.

The same passage from the original notebook, as recounted by B. V. Narasimha Swami, continues: "It is not by a single hearing of the statement that 'I am not the body but the Atman' that the goal is reached. Do we gain a high status simply by seeing a king or a similar person of high rank? One must constantly enter into samadhi and realize one's Self and completely blot out the old vasana-s and the mind before one realizes the Self."

This passage, which is similar to the published version of the text, specifies several points, among these being that a single listening to the spiritual instruction regarding Knowledge of the Self will not, in itself, suffice for Self-Realization; the effort or practice applied is of the nature of entrance into samadhi; that the samadhi is of the nature of realizing one's Self; and that the tendencies and the mind are destroyed prior to complete Realization of the Self.

Merely hearing or reading spiritual instruction will not bring Self-Realization, for such Realization is of the nature of nonobjective Self-Knowledge. Such is immediate experience, that is, direct experience that is nondependent on anything else, such as words and thoughts. Insight acquired from such listening should not be mistaken by the seeker of

Realization as complete Self-Knowledge. This is so even if the intellect is capable of following the reasoning that is characteristic of Vedanta teachings. For Self-Realization, one's own identity must remain absorbed in the Self, without an alternative.

Such absorption is samadhi. Here, the Maharshi's instruction again parallels that of Adi Sankara in *Viveka-cudamani*, and may be given, perhaps in reference to it, especially as found in verses 343, 353, 354, 364, 365, and 366. Verse 343 (verse 342 in some editions) reads:

आरूढशक्तेरहमो विनाशः
    कर्तुं न शक्यः सहसापि पण्डितैः ।
ये निर्विकल्पाख्यसमाधिनिश्चला-
    स्तानन्तरानन्तभवा हि वासनाः ॥

ārūḍhaśakterahamo vināśaḥ
    kartuṁ na śakyaḥ sahasāpi paṇḍitaiḥ |
ye nirvikalpākhyasamādhiniścalā-
    s-tānantarānantabhavā hi vāsanāḥ ||

which may be translated as, "The destruction of the ego that has grown powerful is not possible immediately (or, fortuitously), even by the learned (or, the wise), except for those who are unmoving in undifferentiated samadhi, for, indeed, the tendencies are of endless becomings (or, of many existences)." Verse 353 (verse 352 in some editions) is:

इत्थं विपश्चित्सदसद्विभज्य
    निश्चित्य तत्त्वं निजबोधदृष्ट्या ।
ज्ञात्वा स्वमात्मानमखण्डबोधं
    तेभ्यो विमुक्तः स्वयमेव शाम्यति ॥

itthaṁ vipaścitsadasadvibhajya
    niścitya tattvaṁ nijabodhadṛṣṭyā |
jñātvā svamātmānamakhaṇḍabodhaṁ
    tebhyo vimuktaḥ svayameva śāmyati ||

which may be translated as, "Thus, in this manner, the wise one, separating the real [and] the unreal, ascertaining the Truth by the eye of innate Knowledge (or, his own eye of

Knowledge) having known his own Self [of] partless Knowledge, liberated from them (vasana-s, tendencies), is, of his ownself, alone (or, indeed) peaceful." Verse 354 (353 in some editions) is:

अज्ञानहृदयग्रन्थेर्निःशेषविलयस्तदा ।
समाधिनाविकल्पेन यदाद्वैतात्मदर्शनम् ॥

ajñānahṛdayagrantherniḥśeṣavilayastadā |
samādhināvikalpena yadādvaitātmadarśanam ||

which may be translated as, "Then, there is the complete destruction, without remainder, of the ignorance of the knot of the heart, by samadhi without vikalpa-s (differences, doubts) for one who has the revelation of the nondual Self." Verse 364 (363 in some editions):

समाधिनानेन समस्तवासना
ग्रन्थेर्विनाशोऽखिलकर्मनाशः ।
अन्तर्बाहिः सर्वत एव सर्वदा
स्वरूपविस्फूर्तिरयत्नतः स्यात् ॥

samādhinānena samastavāsanā-
granthervināśo'khilakarmanāśaḥ |
antarbahiḥ sarvata eva sarvadā
svarūpavisphūrtirayatnataḥ syāt ||

which may be translated as, "By this samadhi, there is the complete destruction of the knot of the whole aggregate of vasana-s, and the entire karma is destroyed. Within and without, in every way, indeed, always one's own nature will be flashing forth effortlessly." Verse 365 (364 in some editions):

श्रुतेः शतगुणं विद्यान्मननं मननादपि ।
निदिध्यासं लक्षगुणमनन्तं निर्विकल्पकम् ॥

śruteḥ śataguṇaṁ vidyānmananaṁ mananādapi |
nididhyāsaṁ lakṣaguṇamanantaṁ nirvikalpakam ||

which may be translated as, "Reflection on knowledge is a hundred-fold listening. Meditation, though, is a hundred thousand-fold reflection. The undifferentiated (nirvikalpa) is infinite (limitless)." And verse 366 (365 in some editions):

निर्विकल्पकसमाधिना स्फुटं
ब्रह्मतत्त्वमवगम्यते ध्रुवम् ।
नान्यथा चलतया मनोगतेः
प्रत्ययान्तरविमिश्रितं भवेत् ॥

nirvikalpakasamādhinā sphuṭaṁ
    brahmatattvamavagamyate dhruvam |
nānyathā calatayā manogateḥ
    pratyayāntaravimiśritaṁ bhavet ||

which may be translated as, "By the undifferentiated (nirvikalpa) samadhi, the Brahman-Truth is clearly evident (or, reached, or one is convinced of) with certainty (or, constancy). Otherwise, because of the moving (inconstancy) of the mind's course (or, desires), assumptions (beliefs, conceptions) will become mingled (mixed together) within."

Entrance into samadhi entails dissolution of the misidentifications with anything differentiated from the Absolute. Self-inquiry is such entrance, for it destroys the misidentifications, including the notion, or assumption, of the individual defined by the misidentifications. The nature of the samadhi referred to by the Maharshi, and evident in the cited passages of Adi Sankara, is absorption in Self-Knowledge, which constitutes Self-Realization. In that, knowing and Being are identical. Though this may, at first, be viewed as a state of absorption, by the relinquishment of the very notion of an existent ego, its nature is revealed as indivisible, nondual Being. This is the innate samadhi, and that is eternal, without beginning or end. By the practice of ego-dissolution, which is accomplished by means of Self-inquiry, the tendencies, which are the manifestations of ignorance, are destroyed. The very idea of an existent mind is similarly destroyed. When there is neither tendency nor mind, neither the bondage of ignorance nor the individual to be so bound, such is Self-Realization. The samadhi should be constant, declares Sri Bhagavan. Constancy can never be a bodily state, a sensory state, or a mental state. Constancy lies in that which transcends these. Constancy lies in that which is innate and eternal. Such constancy is the real Self.

174

Such constancy is of the inquiry, for that which liberates one from the mental states and such cannot be of the nature of the mental states and such. The end itself shines as the means. As Brahman, itself, shines as the guru, so the Supreme Knowledge shines as the inquiry.

Whoever inquires in this manner will awaken from the dream of jiva-hood and, free of forgetfulness of his true nature, realizing the Self that has ever been present, and thereby recovering the Bliss that was never lost, realize himself to be Siva. This is infinite Wisdom and Bliss.

Om Sri Ramanarpanamastu
Om May this be an offering to Sri Ramana

38

Disciple: If the jiva is by nature identical with the Self, what is it that prevents the jiva from realizing its true nature?

The Maharshi: It is forgetfulness of the jiva's true nature; this is known as the power of veiling.

Commentary:

Om Namo Bhagavate Sri Ramanaya

The question arises for the aspirant who is keen on knowing the Self: if the jiva is already identical with the Self, what is preventing that jiva from realizing its nature? In other words, if the jiva is not a jiva at all, what is maintaining this delusion, or why does not the Self know itself as it is, utterly devoid of jiva-hood?

The Maharshi's profound answer is succinct and pithy. It is due to the veiling power of ignorance, the sheer forgetfulness of the Self. Ignorance manifests in a two-fold manner: as veiling and as illusory projection of multiplicity. The illusory projection of multiplicity, which has veiling as its cause or root, manifests as thoughts, sensations, the world, etc. These have already been thoroughly dealt with by the Maharshi. By His grace and Truth, all differentiation or multiplicity is negated, leaving only the true Existence as the real remainder. Veiling is merely the not-knowing of the Self manifesting as the inadvertence that brings on misidentification. The veil is of no substance. It appears to be present due to lack of inquiry. Search for it with inquiry, and it is nowhere to be found.

What maintains this veil, this delusion, this jiva? That which is objective—gross, subtle, or mental—does not do so because such is imagined only after the veil or the appearance of the individual, or jiva. The Self does not do so, for it is serene, ever as it is, clear and absolutely one; it does not veil itself from itself. The veil or jiva cannot be self-created or maintained, for such would suppose its pre-existence or assume that delusion is self-existent, which is absurd. Who does so? With such inquiry, the jiva and veil vanish without a trace. Who is forgetful of what? Such inquiry eliminates the forgetfulness.

There is no jiva now, nor has there been, nor will there ever be. There is nothing veiled; nor is there anyone for whom there is a veil. Inquire as the Maharshi instructs, and the Truth of the Self is Self-revealed.

Therefore, in *Saddarshanam*, verse 39, (translation by Sri A. R. Natarajan), the Maharshi later declared, "Thoughts of liberation are only so long as one thinks one is bound. One attains the eternally liberated 'I' by the inquiry, 'For whom is bondage?' Thereafter, how can thought of bondage and freedom arise?"

Whoever abides in the Truth of the Self by the power of inquiry forgets his forgetfulness and, without any veil of ignorance, abides as the infinite Wisdom and Bliss.

Om Sri Ramanarpanamastu
Om May this be an offering to Sri Ramana

39

Disciple: If it is true that the jiva has forgotten itself, how does the "I"-experience arise for all?

The Maharshi: The veil does not completely hide the jiva; it only hides the Self-nature of "I," and projects the "I am the body" notion; but it does not hide the Self's existence, which is "I" and which is real and eternal.

Commentary:

Om Namo Bhagavate Sri Ramanaya

The disciple poses a question concerning, if the jiva is immersed in ignorance characterized by forgetfulness of its own true nature, how can it come to know itself at all? How does the "I-experience" arise for all, when the jiva is steeped in delusion's darkness? How can the light of Knowledge shine at all, even in the form of "I," since the shadow of ignorance is prevailing? Is not maya's veil impenetrable? How can the Self's light shine in the midst of illusion?

The Maharshi's reply reveals the Self's unveiled Existence. This Existence is real and eternal. The unreal cannot hide the real; the nonexistent cannot obscure Existence itself. It is, for all eternity, unmodified, unobscured, shining as the "I" in all beings. It has already been declared by Sri Bhagavan that the jiva is nothing other than Siva. The veil of forgetfulness, manifesting as ignorance in the form of misidentifications, merely projects the false "I-am-the-body" notion. It does nothing at all to the Existence, which is the true nature of the jiva.

The Self is the "I" in each being. "I" is undeniable. Existence is doubtless. If one inquires "Who am I?", the misidentification with the body is destroyed, as well as any other definitions attributed to the "I," such as were described in the context of the five sheaths, the three states, etc. That which stands self-revealed upon this inquiry is the real Self.

Since the jiva is nothing at all in its jiva-ness and is the Self in its true nature, the forgetfulness offers no actual obstruction. The darkness of ignorance is insubstantial, and, in truth, it never prevails. Maya's veil is composed of nothingness. In light of this, the question is not how can the Self come to know itself, but rather how can the Self not know itself? There is no valid reason. The forgetfulness and illusion are merely ignorance, and ignorance has no real cause. Explanations of ignorance are taught in order that one might inquire and discover its unreal nature.

One may think one's position is on one side, the Self on the other, with the veil of illusion between. The pure Truth

177

of Advaita Vedanta causes that perspective to utterly evaporate without leaving so much as a trace. "Is the Self apart? Am I a jiva? What is the veil, and for whom is it? Who am I? Who has forgotten what?" By wisely inquiring in this way, one realizes the Self, the sole-existent Reality. One realizes that there is no veil, no bondage, no one to be bound, and nothing veiled. The Self is real and eternal. That, itself, is the "I"—the only "I" that exists. The sages and scriptures declare it, direct experience proves it, and the Sadguru reveals it.

Therefore, in Adi Sankara's *Vivekacudamani*, we find these verses correlating to the nondual Truth revealed by Sri Bhagavan. Verse 570 (569 in some editions):

मायाक्लृप्तौ बन्धमोक्षौ न स्तः स्वात्मनि वस्तुतः ।
यथा रज्जौ निष्क्रियायां सर्पाभासविनिर्गमौ ॥

m\=ay\=aklptau bandhamoksau na stah sv\=atmani
   vastutah |
yath\=a rajjau niskriy\=ay\=am sarp\=abh\=asavinirgamau ||

which may be translated as: "Conjured (contrived) by illusion are bondage and liberation, which do not exist in the Self, the Reality, just as the mere appearance and disappearance of the snake in the inactive rope." (Alternative interpretation of 570 first line: Conjured by illusion, bondage and liberation, in reality, do not exist in the Self.) Verse 571 (570 in some editions):

आवृतेः सदसत्त्वाभ्यां वक्तव्ये बन्धमोक्षणे ।
नावृतिर्ब्रह्मणः काचिदन्याभावादनावृतम् ।
यद्यस्त्यद्वैतहानिः स्याद्द्वैतं नो सहते श्रुतिः ॥

\=avrteh sadasattv\=abhy\=am vaktavye bandhmoksane |
n\=avrtirbrahmanah k\=a`cidanyabh\=av\=adan\=avrtam |
yadyastyadvaitah\=anih sy\=addvaitam no sahate \'srutih ||

which may be translated as: "If there is the existence and nonexistence of concealment, bondage and liberation may be spoken of. There is no concealment of Brahman whatsoever, for there is no other existence (thing) to conceal it. If there would be, nonduality would be destroyed (obstructed, damaged), yet the Veda-s (Sruti-s) do not allow (endure, approve) duality."

If there is an individual "I" who is bound, there is liberation to be sought. Inquiring, as the Maharshi instructs, as to who is bound, no individual is to be found. Liberation remains as the natural, innate state, the only state there is, for the Self is one without a second. Without any duality of states, the Self alone is, the only Reality for all eternity. No other has ever come to be. Thus, Sri Bhagavan declares the Existence, the Self, to be "real and eternal."

Whoever absorbs this teaching realizes the true nature of "I," and with the disappearance of the veil of the unreal, abides as the Self, which is the eternal, sole-existent Reality, in infinite Wisdom and Bliss.

Om Sri Ramanarpanamastu
Om May this be an offering to Sri Ramana

40

Disciple: What are the characteristics of the jivan-mukta (the liberated in life) and the videha-mukta (the liberated at death)?

The Maharshi: "I am not the body; I am Brahman, which is manifest as the Self. In me who am the plenary Reality, the world consisting of bodies etc., is a mere appearance, like the blue of the sky." He who has realized the truth thus is a jivan-mukta. Yet, so long as his mind has not been resolved, there may arise some misery for him because of relation to objects on account of prarabdha (karma which has begun to fructify and whose result is the present body), and, as the movement of mind has not ceased, there will not be also the experience of bliss. The experience of the Self is possible only for the mind that has become subtle and unmoving as a result of prolonged meditation. He who is thus endowed with a mind that has become subtle and who has the experience of the Self is called a jivan-mukta. It is the state of jivan-mukta that is referred to as the attribute-less Brahman and as the Turiya. When even the subtle mind gets resolved, and experience of self ceases, and when one is immersed in the ocean of bliss and has become one with it without any

179

differentiated existence, one is called a videha-mukta. It is the state of videhamukti that is referred to as the transcendent attributeless Brahman and as the transcendent Turiya. This is the final goal. Because of the grades in misery and happiness, the released ones, the jivan-muktas and videha-muktas, may be spoken of as belonging to four categories: Brahmavid, Brahmavidvara, Brahmavidvariyan, and Brahmavidvarishtha. But these distinctions are from the standpoint of the others who look at them; in reality, however, there are no distinctions in release gained through jnana.

Commentary:

Om Namo Bhagavate Sri Ramanaya

From the standpoint of those who are not realized, pluralism is seen everywhere, even when they attempt to gaze at Realization and realized sages. As Realization is of the Self and the Self is the nondual Reality, there cannot be any divisions, levels, or degrees within it. There are not different kinds of the Self, and therefore, there are not different kinds of Realization. The Self is only one, and Realization is that in which Knowing and Being are one and the same. Yet people, adhering to the delusive belief in a separated individuality, or ego, and attempting to measure by bodily expressions, conceive of stages of Realization. To accommodate them, yet only to lead them on to the nondual Truth, even the scriptures speak of mukti (Liberation) in different forms. They speak of two categories: jivanmukti (Liberation while alive) and videhamukti (disembodied Liberation), often declaring the first leads to the latter. Elsewhere, such as in the *Aksyopanishad,* they speak of the four categories of the knowers of Brahman. *Yoga Vasishtha* (in which Vasistha instructs Rama), *Annapurnopanishad* (in which Ribhu instructs Nidagha), and *Vivekacudamani* deal extensively with these. The reference to the arising of some misery properly refers to one yet practicing nididhyasana (profound meditation), not abiding effortlessly in Self-Realization, perhaps as a comment in accord with verse 446 of *Vivekacudamani.* These same scriptures negate all differences whatsoever, and Sri Adi Sankara, in verses 454 and 455, explicitly negates any consideration of prarabdha for those who abide in the attributeless Brahman, as the Maharshi himself has declared. Even in the explanation of these passages by Sri Ramana, he, for the benefit of the disciple, speaks of jivanmukti in two different ways, with an unresolved mind in relation to objects presented by prarabdha and as unmoving in the experience of the Self. This, then, is declared to be the attributeless Brahman, yet videhamukti—the transcendent, attributeless Brahman—is mentioned thereafter. Sri Ramana declares, "But these distinctions are from the standpoint of the others who look at them; in reality, however, there are no distinctions in release (mukti) gained through jnana (knowledge)." The mukta (liberated one) knows, "I am not the body; I am Brahman, which is the Self. In me who am the perfectly full Reality, the world consisting of bodies, etc., is a mere appearance like the blueness of the sky." Because the disciples see a body, etc., the Maharshi says the jivanmukta sees all this appearance as unreal and abides as Brahman, inwardly silent and blissful even in the midst of outer hardships, the final play of prarabdha karma, and the apparent movement of thought. His state of Bliss may not be evident as it is when such a jivanmukta is seen in meditation, the apparent mind disappearing in its subtlety. When all relative experience ceases in the one undifferentiated Existence, Brahman, and the body with its prarabdha is no more, such is called videhamukti.

The negation of the consideration of prarabdha for the mukta is revealed by Adi Sankara in *Vivekacudamani,* a book to which there are numerous references in this *Self-Inquiry,* in several verses, and among these are verses 455 through 462. Afterward, Sankara explains that teachings in scriptures relating to prarabdha are merely expedient explanations for those who still confound the body with Reality. Verse 455 (454 in some editions):

उपाधितादात्म्यविहीनकेवल-
ब्रह्मात्मनैवात्मनि तिष्ठतो मुनेः ।

प्रारब्धसद्भावकथा न युक्ता
स्वप्नार्थसंबन्धकथेव जाग्रतः ॥

upādhitādātmyavihīnakevala-
　brahmātmanaivātmani tiṣṭhato muneḥ |
prārabdhasadbhāvakathā na yuktā
　svapnārthasambandhakatheva jāgrataḥ ||

which may be translated as: "Devoid of identification with the limitations, the Brahman-Self alone, in the Self alone, is this abidance of the sage. It is not appropriate to discuss the existence of prarabdha, for it is like discussing the connection (association, relationship) of the dream object with the one who is awake." Verse 456 (455 in some editions):

न हि प्रबुद्धः प्रतिभासदेहे
　देहोपयोगिन्यपि च प्रपञ्चे ।
करोत्यहंतां ममतामिदंतां
　किं तु स्वयं तिष्ठति जागरेण ॥

na hi prabuddhaḥ pratibhāsadehe
　dehopayoginyapi ca prapañce|
karotyahaṁtāṁ mamatāmidaṁtāṁ
　kiṁ tu svayaṁ tiṣṭhati jāgareṇa ||

which may be translated as: "Because, one who has awakened is not manifest in (has no similarity to, has not occurring in his mind) the body, and the body is conducive to the diverse manifestation of the defects of 'I,' 'mine,' and 'this,' but, of his own nature, he abides with the wakeful."

Alternative translation: "Not, indeed, is the one who has awakened in the manifest body, although employing the body in the manifestation (that) makes 'I,' 'mine,' and 'this,' but he abides by himself with the wakeful." Verse 457 (456 in some editions):

न तस्य मिथ्यार्थसमर्थनेच्छा न संग्रहस्तज्जगतोऽपि दृष्टः ।
तत्रानुवृत्तिर्यदि चेन्मृषार्थे न निद्रया मुक्त इतीष्यते ध्रुवम् ॥

na tasya mithyārthasamarthanecchā na
saṅgrahastajjagato'pi dṛṣṭaḥ |
tatrānuvṛttiryadi cenmṛṣārthe na nidrayā mukta
itīṣyate dhruvam ||

which may be translated as: "Not for him are the false
objects, the insisting on what is impossible (deliberating on
desire, the force of desire); he is not associated with that
world, the perceived, indeed. If there is the least concept of
those false objects, he is not free from sleep; this is certain."

Alternative translation: "Not for him a false object, or
the insistence on what is impossible according to desire; not
grasping, or the perception of that world, also, perceived, or
imagined, therein, according to the mode (of mind) appearing. If [believing] in the false objects, he is not liberated from
sleep. Thus, it is acknowledged with certainty." Verse 458
(457 in some editions):

तद्वत्परे ब्रह्मणि वर्तमानः सदात्मना तिष्ठति नान्यदीक्षते ।
स्मृतिर्यथा स्वप्नविलोकितार्थे तथा विदः प्राशनमोचनादौ ॥

tadvatpare brahmaṇi vartamānaḥ sadātmanā tiṣṭhati
nānyadīkṣate |
smṛtiryathā svapnavilokitārthe tathā vidaḥ
prāśanamocanādau ||

which may be translated as: "Likewise, attaining abidance in the Absolute Brahman, he abides with his eternal
Self and sees no other. As is the remembrance of objects seen
in a dream, so the knower regards eating, evacuation, and
such." Verse 459 (458 in some editions):

कर्मणा निर्मितो देहः प्रारब्धं तस्य कल्प्यताम् ।
नानादेरात्मनो युक्तं नैवात्मा कर्मनिर्मितः ॥

karmaṇā nirmito dehaḥ prārabdhaṁ tasya kalpyatām |
nānāderātmano yuktaṁ naivātmā karmanirmitaḥ ||

which may be translated as: "By karma, the body is created; prarabdha may be imagined of that. It is not reasonable
to connect such with the beginningless Self, for the Self is,
indeed, not a creation of karma."

Verse 460 (459 in some editions):

अजो नित्यः शाश्वत इति ब्रूते श्रुतिरेषा त्वमोघवाक् ।
तदात्मना तिष्ठतोऽस्य कुतः प्रारब्धकल्पना ॥

ajo nityaḥ śāśvata iti brūte śrutireṣā tvamoghavāk |
tadātmanā tiṣṭhato'sya kutaḥ prārabdhakalpanā ||

(some editions omit śāśvata), which may be translated as: "The unborn, the eternal, the perpetual (constant), thus proclaims the Sruti-s (Veda-s), that, indeed, of infallible speech. From where (how) can there be the imagination of prarabdha for one who abides as that Self?" Verse 461 (460 and part of 461 in some editions):

प्रारब्धं सिध्यति तदा यदा देहात्मना स्थितिः ।
देहात्मभावो नैवेष्टः प्रारब्धं त्यज्यतामतः ।
शरीरस्यापि प्रारब्धकल्पना भ्रान्तिरेव हि ॥

prārabdhaṁ sidhyati tadā yadā dehātmanā sthitiḥ |
dehātmabhāvo naiveṣṭaḥ prārabdhaṁ tyajyatāmataḥ |
śarīrasyāpi prārabdhakalpanā bhrāntireva hi ||

which may be translated as: "Prarabdha is established (accomplished) so long as the stand is the body is the Self. Not, indeed, is valid the concept of the body is the Self, so prarabdha should be abandoned. The imagination of prarabdha of the body, also, is confusion (error, false opinion), certainly." Verse 462 (461 in some editions):

अध्यस्तस्य कुतः सत्त्वमसत्त्वस्य कुतो जनिः ।
अजातस्य कुतो नाशः प्रारब्धमसतः कुतः ॥

adhyastasya kutaḥ sattvamasattvasya kuto janiḥ |
ajātasya kuto nāśaḥ prārabdhamasataḥ kutaḥ ||

which may be translated as: "Of the superimposed (the falsely attributed, the supposed), how (from where) can there be existence (reality)? Of the unreal (nonexistent), how is there birth? Of the unborn, how is there destruction? How (whence) can the unreal prarabdha be?" Alternative translation: "Of the unreal how can prarabdha be?"

What, though, is the Truth of Liberation (Mukti)? "To meet the needs of various seekers Master Ramana did expound various doctrines; we have heard him say that his true teaching firmly based on his own experience is Ajata (no creation, no birth)," Sri Muruganar has proclaimed in the *Garland of Guru's Sayings* (Guru Vachaka Kovai). For the realized sage, there is no jivanmukti and videhamukti; there is only mukti. In one sense, to combine "jiva" and "mukti" could be said to be a contradiction in terms for jiva signifies an illusory bound individual and mukti (Liberation, Release) is characterized by the complete absence of a jiva; but the term is utilized to show that complete Liberation can be realized in life, here and now. Liberation is abidance as the Self, Brahman. Brahman is homogeneous and nondual. There are no individual knowers of Brahman, let alone four kinds. Brahman alone exists and alone knows itself. He who has realized Brahman is Brahman without any distinctions whatsoever. He is not alive, and he is not dead. He is neither with a body nor without a body. He is without any of the three types of karma, says Sri Bhagavan, just as, when a man with three wives dies, all of them are widows. For, as when the snake is seen to be only a rope and not even a trace of anything else, it is not just the head or the tail or the middle that disappears, but the whole of it completely vanishes, because it is entirely unreal and that which is real is now perceived. This Truth about Liberation was reiterated by Sri Bhagavan in *Saddarshanam*, verse 40, (translation by Sri A. R. Natarajan) thus: "Some scholars say that after Liberation form remains. Others say that forms do not last. Yet others say, sometimes form remains and sometimes it is lost. The loss of ego that examines these three concepts alone is true Liberation."

The attributeless Brahman cannot become more so. It is as it is for all eternity. It cannot be described in terms of external appearances. There is, then, no jivanmukti or videhamukti, but only mukti. There has been no bondage, nor is there any now, nor will there be any in the future, for nothing other than the Self, Brahman, has ever come to be. The realized sage has no degrees and no stages, no notion of with or without a body. He sees no world or sentient beings, but only Brahman, the one Existence. He sees that there are none bound, none striving for Liberation, and none liberated. The Self alone exists, ever, and he is that Self alone. There is no state of bondage and no state of liberation; there exists just the Self in its innate, natural state. That alone is. That is the mukta or Self-Realized sage. That is Brahman. That is Jnana or Self-Realization. That is what is revealed by this inquiry into the Self so lovingly taught by the ever-gracious, perfect guru, Bhagavan Sri Ramana Maharshi. His disciples and devotees can never be too grateful to him. What he has revealed, what he causes them to realize, the state in which they who thus inquire abide, and what in Truth they are, is infinite Wisdom and Bliss.

OM TAT SAT

Obeisance

May the Feet of Ramana, the Master, who is the great Siva Himself and is also in human form, flourish forever!

Sri Ramana it is who has revealed all Wisdom and Bliss. The Infinite Himself has revealed the Infinite, the Eternal the Eternal.

May all abide in that Grace and Truth forever. Obeisance again and again to the perfect Guru, Bhagavan Sri Ramana Maharshi.

Om Sri Ramanarpanamastu

GLOSSARY

ADHARAS: Mystic centers.

ADI SANKARA: Also called Sri Sankara; a great Sage who expounded pure Advaita Vedanta frequently mentioned by the Maharshi.

ADVAITA: Not two; nondual; nonduality.

AGAMA-S: A class of scriptures considered divinely revealed, but other than the Veda-s. They are the foundation of ritual and temple worship.

AHAM: I am.

AHAMKARA: Ego; "I" sense.

AHIMSA: Non-injury.

AJAPA: Unuttered, repeated internally japa (i.e., repetition of a mantra). Usually referring to So'ham, "He am I."

AKSHARA-MANA-MALAI: "The Marital Garland of Letters," profound devotional text of 108 verses composed by Sri Bhagavan in about 1914 while he was still in Virupaksa Cave.

AKSHARA: A letter; imperishable.

ANANDAMAYA: Composed of bliss; anandamaya kosa is the sheath of bliss.

ANNAMAYA: Composed of gross matter; annamaya kosa is the sheath of "food" or matter, i.e., the physical body.

APARIGRAHA: Non-possession.

APAROKSANUBHUTI: "The Direct Experience of Reality," a work on Advaita by Sri Adi Sankara.

ARDHA-MATRA: Half-measure, half syllable.

ARUNACHALA: lit. "red mountain," "red and unmoving;" holy hill where Sri Bhagavan dwelt, regarded as a symbol of Siva.

ASANA: Posture; seat; sitting.

ASTAVAKRA: lit., "eight curves;" great sage of ancient times who was the guru of King Janaka.

ASTEYA: Non-stealing.

ATMABODHA: Name of an Upanishad of the *Rig Veda;* title of work by Sri Adi Sankara, i.e., "Self-Knowledge."

ATMALOKA: World of the Self.

ATMASAKSHATKARA: The title of an essential part of an Agama entitled *Sarva Jnanottara;* "Realization of the True Nature of the Self."

AVIDYA: Ignorance; nescience; non-knowledge.

BHADRA: Name of asana; blessed; auspicious; fortunate; happy; excellent; skilful.

BHAGAVAD G1TA: Famous Hindu scripture in which Lord Sri Krishna instructs Arjuna; lit. "Song of God."

BHAKTA: Devotee.

BHUTA: Gross element.

BRAHMARANDHRA: Aperture in crown of the head.

BRAHMACHARYA: Celibacy; defined by the Maharshi to mean "Dwelling in Brahman."

BRAHMAVID: Knower of Brahman.

BUDDHI: Intellect; mind.

CHAKRA: Wheel; a subtle center of subtle body.

CHANDOGYA: Name of an Upanisad from the *Sama Veda.*

CHITTA: Mind; memory.

DAHARA-VIDYA: Meditation on, or Knowledge of, God in the space of the Heart.

DAKSHINAMURTI: Primordial Guru; Siva incarnate; symbol of pure Jnana and Absolute Silence; lit. "southward facing," though the Maharshi once interpreted it as "wisely functioning formlessness."

DARSHAN (DARSAN, DARSHANAM): Vision; seeing; revelation.

DATTATREYA: A great sage of ancient times, the Avadhuta, to whom is ascribed *Avadhuta Gita* and who appears in *Tripura Rahasya.*

DEVIKALOTTARA: Title of minor Agama translated by Sri Bhagavan.

DHARANA: Concentration of the mind.

DHYANA: Meditation.

DHYANABINDU: Name of an Upanisad of the *Krishna Yajur Veda.*

DRIK: Knower; seer.

DRISYA: Known; object; seen.

GANAPATI: Lord or chief of the Gana-s (Siva's retinue); another name of Ganesa.

GAUDAPADA: Adi Sankara's Guru's Guru.

GAYATRI MANTRA: Said to be the most sacred of Vedic mantras, in a Vedic meter described as consisting of 24 syllables, but variants of the number of syllables in the meter range from 19-26. The mantra is:

> Om bhur bhuvah svah
> tat savitur varenyam
> bhargo devasya dhimahi
> dhiyo yo nah pracodayat.

GUNA-S. Guna means quality; attribute; characteristic. There are three guna-s.

1. sattva: buoyant, illuminating, light, knowledge, happiness

2. rajas: agitation, stimulating, mobile, pain, action

3. tamas: heavy, enveloping, dark, indifferent, laziness, inertia

Guna also means a rope; the three constituents are said to be like strands of a rope that bind the individual.

HAMSA (HAMSA MANTRA): The mantra So'ham naturally uttered with every breath; also the name of an Upanishad.

HARI: Vishnu.

HASTAMALAKA: Disciple of Sri Adi Sankara.

HRIDAYAM: Heart.

HRIT-AYAM: "Heart I am."

ISVARA-PRANIDHANA: Devotion to God.

ISVARA: The Lord.

JAGAT-JIVA-PARA: The world-the individual-the Supreme.

JANAKA: One of several sagely kings; disciple of Ashtavakra.

JIVA: Individual; individual soul; life.

JIVANMUKTA: One who is liberated while alive; a sage.

JIVATMAN: Individual self.

JNANA: Knowledge; wisdom.

JNANENDRIYA: Organs of knowledge, especially the senses.

JNANI: One who has jnana, Knowledge; a Self-Realized sage.

KAILASA: The abode of Siva; a mountain in the Himalayas of that name.

KAIVALYA: The state of abidance as That which alone is.

KARANA: Causal; karana sarira is the causal body.

KARIKA: A type of commentary, most notably Gaudapada's Karika on *Mandukya Upanishad*.

KARMENDRIYA: Organs of action.

KENA: Name of an Upanishad of the *Sama Veda*.

KEVALA: The one; the lone; adjective form of Kaivalya(m).

KOSA: Sheath.

KRISHNA (KRSNA): A great sage of antiquity who revealed his Teachings in *Bhagavad Gita, Uttara Gita,* and *Uddhava Gita*. Regarded as the very incarnation of Vishnu.

KUMBHAKA: Cessation or retention of the breath.

MAHA-RISHI: Great sage, usually combined as maharshi.

MAHABHARATA: The great epic within which appears the *Bhagavad Gita*.

MAHANARAYANA: Name of an Upanishad.

MAHATATTVA: "Great intellect"—the projected light from Absolute Consciousness.

MAHAVAKYA: Great saying; great aphorism; specifically four aphorisms, drawn from one Veda each, declaring the identity of the Self and Brahman.

MAHAYOGI: The great yogi; name of Siva.

MALA: Impurity.

MALA: Garland.

MANOMAYA: Composed of the mind; manomaya kosa is the sheath of the mind.

MANONASA: Destruction of the mind; extinction of the mind.

MANTRA: Sacred formula, hymn, or incantation.

MAUNAKSHARA: Silent syllable; imperishable Silence.

MAYA: Illusion, delusion.

MANDUKYA; MANDUKYOPANISHAD: An Upanishad pertaining to the *Atharva Veda,* upon which Sri

Gaudapada, Sri Adi Sankara's Guru's Guru, wrote a nondual commentary *(Karika)*.

MOKSHA: Liberation; release; spiritual freedom.

MURTI: Form; specifically a representation of a deity.

MUNDAKA: Name of an Upanishad from *Atharva Veda.*

NACHIKETA: Central figure of *Katha Upanishad.*

NADA: Subtle sound.

NADI: Subtle nerve (lit. vessel).

NAISHKARMYASIDDHI: Work on Advaita composed by Sri Suresvaracarya, who is a disciple of Sri Adi Sankara

NAMAH: Salutation.

NAMAVALI: Refers to a set of names, usually 108 in number, for use for worship such as in puja, that describe the one who is worshipped, e.g., *Sri Ramana Ashtottara, The 108 Names of Sri Ramana;* An adornment of names.

NATARAJA: Siva; the king of the dance.

NETI: "Not this."

NIDAGHA: Disciple of Ribhu; his name means "to consume by fire."

MUKTI: Liberation; release.

NIDIDHYASANA: Profound meditation.

NIYAMA: Observances.

OMKARA: Om, the sound or written symbol, or written word "Om."

PADMA: Lotus; name of asana.

PADMAPADA: "Lotus foot;" disciple of Sri Adi Sankara.

PANCHAKSHARA: Five syllabled, specifically the five syllable mantra "Namah Sivaya."

PANCIKARANA: Quintuplication of elements. The world is said to be formed by the five elements by a process of each of the elements combining with the others in various proportions.

PARABHAKTI: Supreme devotion.

PARAMAPADA: The feet of the Supreme; the Supreme State.

PARAMATMAN: Supreme Self.

PRAHLADA: As depicted in *Yoga Vasistha,* an Asura or Daitya who became enlightened after he received the boon of being able to practice Self-inquiry.

PRAJNANA: Supreme Knowledge; Consciousness.

PRAKRITI: Manifestation.

PRANA: Vital air, life breath, vitality, life energy; said to be divided into 5 or 10 kinds or functions.

PRANAMAYA: Composed of the prana or vital air; prana-maya kosa is the sheath of prana.

PRANAVA: Om, Aum; The word "Om."

PRANAYAMA: Control of prana, usually associated with breath control.

PRARABDHA: Karma as the residue of results of acts that has fructified and started working itself out during the present life.

PRATYAHARA: Drawing back or withdrawal, especially of the senses from external objects; dissolution of the world; withdrawal from the senses; defined in *Self-Inquiry* in terms of Jnana, as well.

PUJA: Worship; adoration; homage.

PURAKA: Inhalation; filling.

PURANA: A particular kind of Hindu text, consisting of ancient lore, encyclopedic in nature, said to be 18 in number, composed by Sage Vyasa.

RAJA: King.

RAJAS: Same as rajo-guna

RAJO-GUNA: The quality of excitement, agitation, pain.

RECHAKA: Exhalation.

RIBHU GITA: "Song of Ribhu"—a great text of Advaita in which Ribhu enlightens Nidagha, very often mentioned by the Maharshi.

RISHI (RSI): Sage.

RUDRA: Siva; Siva as destruction; "He who drives away suffering;" "praiseworthy;" "having or bestowing power."

RUDRASAMHITA: Portion of *Siva Purana*.

SADGURU: The true guru (who reveals the Truth).

SADHANA: Spiritual practice.

SAHAJA: Natural; effortless; innate state.

SAIVITE: Pertaining to Saivism, or the religion of Siva.

SAKSHI: The witness.

SAMADHI: State of absorption, union, meditation in which one is identified with that upon which one meditates.

SAMANYA: Common; general; with same theme; a class of Upanishad dealing with Vedanta.

SAMARASA: Having the same essence, having equal feeling.

SAMSARA: Cycle of birth and death, transmigration; worldly life.

SANAKA: Rishi, disciple of Dakshinamurti.

SANANDANA: Rishi, disciple of Dakshinamurti.

SANAT KUMARA: Rishi, disciple of Dakshinamurti.

SANAT SUJATA: Rishi, disciple of Dakshinamurti.

SANNYASA (SAMNYASA): Renunciation.

SANNYASIN (SANNYASI): Renouncer.

SANTOSHA: Contentment.

SARVANGA: All aspects; all limbs; all divisions.

SATTVA-GUNA: The quality of balance; inclined toward Knowledge; illuminating.

SATYA: Truth; truthfulness.

SAUCHA: Purity.

SAVIKALPA: Determinate; a type of samadhi in which the mind is functioning and distinctions such as knower, knowledge, and knowing remain.

SANKALPA (SAMKALPA): Mental resolve; will; volition; thought; desire; wish; idea; imagination.

SIDDHA: Accomplished one; one who displays miraculous power; name of asana.

SIDDHANTA: "Settled conclusion;" a Saivite philosophy.

SIMHA: "Lion;" name of Asana.

SIVA: The Good, the Auspicious, the Absolute.

SKANDOPANISHAD: An Upanishad of the *Krishna Yajurveda,* considered one of the Samanya Vedanta Upanishads.

SO'HAM: "He am I."

STULA SAR1RA: Physical body.

SUJATA (SANAT SUJATA) Rishi, disciple of Dakshina-murti.

SUKSHMA (SUKSMA): Subtle.

SURESVARA: Disciple of Sri Adi Sankara.

SURESVARACARYA: The great teacher, Suresvara, disciple of Sri Adi Sankara.

SVADHYAYA: Study of sacred texts.

SVETAKETU: Son of Uddalaka; he receives the instruction of "you are That"—tat tvam asi—in *Chandogya Upanishad.*

TAIJASA-JIVA: Dream state experiencer.

TAITTIRIYA: Name of an Upanishad from the *Krishna Yajur Veda.*

TAMAS: Dullness; darkness; inertia; heavy.

TAMO-GUNA: The quality of darkness, dullness, or inertia.

TANMATRA: Subtle essences (of the 5 elements, considered in connection with the 5 senses).

TANTRA-S: Rules, rituals, and religious treatises for modes of worship; doctrine or treatise teaching magical or mystical formulas for worship and attainment of superhuman powers.

TAPAS: Penance; religious austerity; mortification; meditation connected with the practice of personal self-denial or bodily mortification; moral virtue; merit; special duty or observance of any particular caste. Tapah means heat; warmth; fire; the sun; the hot season and the like. Tapas has been translated also as intense, fiery practice.

TAPASVI: One who observes tapas.

TARBODHAM: Self-conceit.

TAT: That.

TATTVA: Factor of experience; Truth.

TEJO-BINDOPANISHAD: An Upanishad of the *Krishna Yajur Veda.*

TIRTHA: A passage; way; ford; bathing place; place of pilgrimage; right moment.

TOTAKA: Disciple of Sri Adi Sankara.

TRIPURA RAHASYA: A nondual south Indian scripture referred to by the Maharshi and authored by Haritayana, who is associated with the Minakshi temple in Madurai.

TURIYA: The fourth (state).

TURIYATITA: Beyond the fourth (state).

UDDALAKA: Father of Svetaketu: he gave the instruction "you are That"—tat tvam asi—in *Chandogya Upanishad.*

UPADESA: Spiritual instruction.

UPANISHAD: lit. "sitting near, devotedly;" the instruction received by sitting near the Guru (which gives) certitude and cleanses (sorrow); that which reveals the Knowledge of Brahman, secret teaching; Knowledge of the Absolute; the concluding portion of the Veda-s.

VAIKUNTHA: The abode of Vishnu.

VASANA-S: Tendencies; residual impressions.

VASISTHA: Great sage from ancient times. Guru of Rama in *Yoga Vasistha,* a great scripture of Advaita Vedanta.

VEDANTA CHUDAMANI: Text on Vedanta.

VICHARASANGRAHAM: "A Compendium of Inquiry;" the title of this book, usually translated simply as "Self-Inquiry."

VIDEHA-MUKTA: One who is liberated without the body.

VIDEHA-MUKTI: Liberation without the body.

VIDYA: Knowledge.

VIJNANA: Knowledge; intelligence; discernment; understanding.

VIJNANAKOSA: Sheath of the intellect.

VIJNANAMAYA: Composed of the intellect; vijnanamaya kosa is the sheath of the intellect.

VIKALPA: Imagination; mental concept; misapprehension; misconception; differentiation; doubt.

VIKARA: Change; change of form.

VIRUPAKSA: "Having diverse or odd eyes;" name of Siva referring to His having 3 eyes; the name of a cave on Arunachala where the Maharshi lived.

YANTRA: Mystic diagram, usually of geometric pattern(s), used for meditation.

YOGIN: Same as yogi; practitioner of yoga.

VISHNU: A name of God; the all-pervading.

VISVA: Waking; visva-jiva is the waking state experiencer.

VIVEKACUDAMANI: "The Crest Jewel of Discrimination," the title of a work on Advaita Vedanta by Adi Sankara, which was often referenced by the Maharshi.

VRTTI: Mode; modification; thought; notion.

YAJNA; YAGA: Types of sacrificial rites or worship; may also be applied to any pious or devotional act or spiritual offering or endeavor.

Made in the USA
Coppell, TX
14 May 2021